G000060268

A TALE OF NINE CENTURIES

Úna Collins and Sean Goan

A TALE OF NINE
CENTURIES

THE STORY AND SPIRITUALITY OF THE LE CHÉILE
SCHOOLS TRUST

the columba press

First published in 2014 by
the columba press
55A Spruce Avenue,
Stillorgan Industrial Park,
Blackrock, Co. Dublin

Cover by sin é design
Cover image from iStockphoto
Origination by The Columba Press
Printed in Ireland by Sprintprint Ltd

ISBN 9781 78218 131 6

This publication is protected under the Copyright and Related
Rights Act 2000. Conditional to statutory exceptions, no part of
this work may be reproduced without the express permission of
The Columba Press.

The moral rights of the authors have been asserted.

Copyright © 2014, Úna Collins and Sean Goan

TABLE OF CONTENTS

ABOUT THE AUTHORS

Born in Dublin, DR ÚNA COLLINS was educated by the Holy Faith Sisters in Glasnevin and entered the convent at the age of seventeen. Úna graduated with an honours degree in History and English from UCD in 1963 and was awarded an M.Ed in Counselling in Loyola University, Los Angeles in 1971.

During Úna's many years in education she has been in the roles of teacher, guidance counsellor, deputy principal, director of pastoral care in schools, principal, co-ordinator of Holy Faith schools, chairperson of school boards of management, trustee representative for the Holy Faith Congregation, researcher and author. Her primary role has been, and is, that of a religious sister. Her publications include *Pastoral Care and School Behaviour* (1995) and *Developing a School Plan* (1996), both Mario Institute of Education, Dublin and *Rethinking Pastoral Care* (1999) edited with Jean McNiff, Routledge, London.

Úna is still active in school Boards of Management, is a trustee member of the Association of Trusts of Catholic Schools (ATCS), and has engaged with and supported the contemporary research work of Catholic School Partnership (CSP).

Born in Belfast, SEAN GOAN has studied Scripture in Rome and Jerusalem. In addition to teaching, he conducts retreats and reflection days on biblical themes. Sean is currently the Faith Development Officer for the Le Chéile Schools Trust. His previous publications include *Let the Reader Understand: Year A* (2007); *Year B* (2005); *Year C* (2006), all Columba Press and *Exploring Faith: Junior Certificate R.E. Textbook* (2004), Celtic Press.

INTRODUCTION

Confucius, the Chinese philosopher, advises that a study of the past is necessary for those who wish to define the future. This book is about past, present and future. The Le Chéile Catholic Schools Trust was established in contemporary time, but is rooted in the past and is defining and ensuring the future of the Irish Catholic secondary school.

The Trust is unique in its origin. Twelve small religious congregations came together in 2003 and collaborated for seven years to create a new lay Trust which was launched by President McAleese in 2010. The Trust now represents fourteen religious congregations, fifty-nine schools, 1,650 staff members, and 28,684 students.

The Le Chéile story stretches from the twelfth to the twenty-first century and from the United States of America through Italy, France and England to Ireland. It is a story which includes the fascinating lives of a thirteenth-century young nobleman challenging heresy, a nineteenth-century American separated mother of five providing schools for England's young girls, a young bishop learning how to provide Catholic education in an impoverished penal Ireland by observing children sing and play, an Irish woman in prison planning how to educate poor children, and an Anglican nurse in the Crimea converted by the faith of dying Irish soldiers. Each of the fourteen stories is compelling, each one a personal story of a courageous response in faith to the immediate needs of context and time.

This is the story which lies at the heart of the Le Chéile Catholic Schools Trust, the story that gives the Trust its lifeblood and heritage. The name 'Le Chéile', meaning 'together', was chosen in 2003 when the congregations began working together. This is a re-telling in contemporary time of the stories of the founders of the twelve initial congregations and two further congregations which joined the Trust since 2003. Fourteen unique and inspiring stories indicate the founding values of the collaborative Trust and provide the basis for the unique story of the Le Chéile community of schools and a relevant spirituality for our day. Community and spirituality are dynamic and ever-developing but they come from and rest on founding values and heritage.

HISTORICAL CONTEXT

The story begins with Dominic de Guzmán in the twelfth century and is continuing at this present time as Le Chéile prepares to open the first Catholic post-primary school in Ireland for twenty-five years. The nine women and five men who founded the Le Chéile religious congregations have left a spiritual heritage which in contemporary time motivated their members to collaborate and ensure that – as numbers decreased and membership was aging – their Catholic schools in Ireland could continue into the future. Ireland's political, social, educational and religious history is the larger context for both the founding of the Irish congregations and the establishment of Catholic secondary schools by congregations founded in other countries.

The historical, educational, and religious context has a focal point in the sixteenth century when Tudor policy decreed that Irish schools would be used to spread the influence of the Church of England, which had been established during the Reformation. Thus Irish people had their first experience of education promoted and provided by government. Parish schools, diocesan schools and a University (Trinity College), were the chosen instruments to make the Irish people 'English' and 'Protestant'.

Moving from Tudor into Penal Ireland in the eighteenth century we learn that the Irish responded to English laws by providing

Catholic education for their children in hidden 'hedge schools'. These schools were illegal, but they managed to function and survive in many parts of the country. The English Penal State provision of schools was a continuation of the Tudor policy and the practice of proselytism.

The Schools of the Incorporated Society for Promoting English Protestant Schools in Ireland, the Charter Schools, were a network of residential schools across Ireland, with nurseries to feed the schools, and these schools continued to dominate the Irish educational process until the end of the eighteenth century. The Penal Laws' period and, later, the incremental Catholic Relief Acts merged into nineteenth century agrarian conflict and famine. The resulting extremes of poverty were stark and motivated the founders in the Le Chéile stories to educate poor Irish Catholic children.

Interestingly, and at the same time as the Famine and its destructive poverty, many resilient Irish Catholics were developing into a distinct middle class, with potential leadership for political, legal, economic and educational development. The nineteenth century also brought another wave of proselytism. This new wave, which reflected the penal legislation from the sixteenth to the nineteenth century, was driven by a strong evangelical missionary spirit which emerged from a reforming Church of England, and its work in Ireland was supported by English finance. Daniel O' Connell, the great Irish Catholic liberator and orator, specifically addressed the issue when speaking to the members of the movement in 1820. He argued and pleaded with them to recognise the divisive nature of proselytism. His plea was ignored and this practice of religious conversion flourished. This proved to be a motivating force for the founding of indigenous Irish religious congregations.

The new Irish foundations were made mainly by laypeople who subsequently founded religious congregations. Their mission was rooted in the defence and development of faith, and they founded schools to serve this mission. All fourteen congregations responded firstly to those who were most in need. They also provided for the education and faith needs of the children of the middle class.

Religious congregations from France and England came to Ireland to increase that provision.

Le Chéile Congregations

Religious congregations have their origin in the responses of very ordinary, usually lay, people feeling passionately about the needs of the people of their time. Their faith and their generosity of spirit led them to gather others to assist them to meet identified needs. They believed that God wanted them to respond to these needs, and this belief is what is understood as religious vocation. Church history informs us that the Holy Spirit gifts such groups with a specific charism. The members of religious congregations have a responsibility for this charism and for the heritage received from founding members.

The fourteen people whose stories are being woven into Le Chéile are:

- Dominic de Guzmán, a twelfth-century Spanish cleric (founder of the Dominican family);

- Angela de Merici, a fifteenth-century Italian woman (founder of the Ursuline Sisters);

- John Baptist de La Salle, a seventeenth-century French Canon (founder of the De La Salle Brothers);

- Daniel Delaney, an eighteenth-century Irish Bishop, educated and trained in France (founder of the Patrician Brothers);

- Claudine Thévenet, an eighteenth-century young French laywoman (founder of the Religious of Jesus and Mary);

- Anne-Marie Javouhey, an eighteenth-century young French woman (founder of the St Joseph of Cluny Sisters);

- Marie-Madeleine d'Houët, an eighteenth/nineteenth-century young French widow, and mother of one child (founder of the Faithful Companions of Jesus);

- LOUIS LAFOSSE, a nineteenth-century French priest (founder of the Religious of Christian Education);

- LOUIS BAUTAIN, a nineteenth-century French priest (founder of the St Louis Sisters);

- GENEVIEVE DUPUIS, a nineteenth-century French nun (founder of the Sisters of Charity of St Paul the Apostle);

- FRANCES TAYLOR, a nineteenth-century young woman and English convert (founder of the Poor Servants of the Mother of God);

- ELIZABETH PROUT, a nineteenth-century young woman and English convert (founder of the Cross and Passion Sisters);

- CORNELIA CONNELLY, a nineteenth-century American convert and separated mother of five children (founder of the Society of the Holy Child);

- MARGARET AYLWARD, a nineteenth-century Irish middle-aged laywoman (founder of the Holy Faith Sisters).

These women and men believed that they were called by God to dedicate their lives to the people of their time and place, and to found religious congregations in the service of faith and of education. Their stories are now Le Chéile stories, their values are inherited values and their congregational spiritualities are in the process of being woven together to provide a contemporary spirituality for the Le Chéile Schools Trust.

It is in the light of history that we can understand the Le Chéile Schools Trust and within that light we invite the reader to enter into these compelling stories. In the stories we engage with the values and spirituality which emerge, and we also gain an understanding of the contemporary unique story of fourteen congregations collaborating because they were motivated by these values and they formed a new lay trust for their schools. Faith and education are at the centre of the founding stories and are the motivating values for the collaborative trust.

Founding the Le Chéile Trust

The Catholic school is the medium for mission chosen today by the Le Chéile congregations, and a lay trust is the system they chose for the legal, financial, and moral ownership of their Catholic schools. The contemporary historical context of the trusteeship of the Catholic school in Ireland is critical in understanding the decision made by the Le Chéile congregations to ensure the future of their schools by developing a collaborative trust.

In September 2003 members of the initial twelve religious congregations gathered in Manresa Centre, Dublin, to face the daunting challenges involved in the planning for the future of their schools. They were twelve small congregations that knew they could not financially afford to establish individual school trusts. They had attended several meetings organised by the Conference of Religious of Ireland (CORI) and had listened to experts on the legal issues and practical responsibilities regarding future trusteeship. Decision time had arrived. Central to that decision was the question of maintaining individual founding values, and the heritage and identity of the schools of each congregation. Another consideration was how school communities might respond to the loss of their own historic congregational identity. After two days of discussion and reflection a decision had not been made and the underlying questions were not answered. The facilitator suggested that two representatives of each congregation would take time out to identify which founding value had to be recognised by all so that the congregation could move further in the collaborative process. When the congregational members regrouped and the individual congregational core values were identified there were some moments of silence and awe. The congregational representatives were recognizing what should have been obvious, that all congregational core values are rooted in the gospel value of proclaiming and teaching the redemptive love of God, and they identified their individual founding values in that gospel context.

In what came to be known by the congregational representatives as the 'Manresa moment' a unique collaborative schools trust was conceived in 2003. The representatives left the meeting with the intention of reporting to their congregational leaders and with an agreement to meet again in October. This was the group of people who would continue to represent the congregations in developing the new Trust. The group would be known as the Le Chéile Working Group, and it met on the first Friday of each month for seven years. The new Trust was launched in 2010. The name 'Le Chéile' was chosen in 2004 as the Trust began to take its initial shape, and as its charter was being written. The St Joseph of Cluny congregation joined the emerging Trust in 2009 and the Ursuline congregation joined the established Trust in 2012–13.

On Friday, 5 February 2010, the religious congregations with their schools' staffs and students celebrated the launch of the Le Chéile Catholic Schools Trust in Dublin. After the seven years of intense collaborative work they became one community of faith and of learning while still maintaining their individual congregational identities. The religious congregations had invested their school property and significant finance in the Trust. More importantly they invested the heritage of their founders. They were motivated by one clear goal, to ensure that the Irish Catholic secondary schools, for which they had responsibility, would continue into the future.

The collaborative story is unique in the long and varied history of Catholic schooling in Ireland, and in particular, the history of the Irish Catholic post-primary school. The Le Chéile Working Group, members of each of the twelve founding congregations, brought to the seven-year process their educational and congregational leadership experience. With the expert guidance of Dr David Tuohy sj the group engaged in the remits and implications of civil and canon law. The schools' principals and boards of management were involved in all decisions and developments, and continue to be centrally engaged as company members of the Trust.

Each of the congregations has its unique history and heritage. This historical identity will, it is hoped, be a source of inspiration and strength for Le Chéile Trust as it develops. However, it is also the right of each congregational school to know about and to own the richness of the other histories and heritages now shared within the Trust. The Trust provides the sixty schools with a loom and shuttle to begin weaving each unique thread of congregational heritage into a single Le Chéile tapestry. In this new reality the schools can recognise a Le Chéile identity, and can develop a spirituality which is enriched by the values of each of the congregational founding stories.

When President Mary McAleese addressed the gathering at the launch of the new Trust in 2010 she said:

> The founding congregations have come together in a very positive and proactive way creating new clusters of collaborative endeavour which will ensure that the schools cannot only continue into the future, but can do so dynamically and energetically fired by the charisms and rich cultures which each congregation represents but also driven by the synergies that Le Chéile offers.

The President was articulating the mission of the Le Chéile religious congregations in their decision to collaborate with each other to ensure the future of their schools. Le Chéile schools are now blessed with fourteen charisms, and with a distinctive new richness of collaboration and community.

At the launch of the Le Chéile Trust girls and boys, students from each congregational grouping of schools, and from every part of the country, sang the new Le Chéile song reflecting the founding mission of Le Chéile, the words of the President of Ireland, and their own youthful, hopeful ownership of the new reality:

Every heart, every voice
Everyone come sing together
As we welcome the dawn of this day.
Here our lives find new beginnings
As we gather giving praise
To the risen Christ who guides us on our way.

Together we will join as one family in Christ,
Sharing gifts as we build a better way.
As we journey on this path united we hold fast
A new beginning, a new day.
His name His word we now proclaim
A new beginning, a new day.

Together we will form one community of faith,
Unified in God's glory we will stay
Disciples of Christ.

This *one community of faith* is the community of schools in the Le Chéile Trust. Within each founding story we can search for what we believe the founder would want the Le Chéile schools to know about their lives, why they founded schools, and what they would say if they were to visit the Le Chéile schools in contemporary Ireland. The founding stories are drawn from the past for a present that is building a future in the schools.

READING THE STORIES TODAY

Irish history is the context for locating the ecclesial, social, economic and educational cultures within which the Le Chéile Irish congregational founding values are to be understood, and within which the international congregations established schools in Ireland. It is of interest to reflect on the historical context of the founding of each congregation. Everyone loves a story and history is the stuff of stories. Historians remind us that the past has made us what we are, and Aristotle advised us that if we wished to understand anything we should observe its beginning and its development. As we move into the fourteen stories of the Le Chéile religious congregations the historical context will help us to understand why these women and men dedicated their lives to God, why they founded congregations to do a particular work, and why their contemporary sisters and brothers, with new lay leaders, want to ensure that the original values are contemporary and operative in the schools in Ireland.

This move from the past to the present with an eye on the future seeks to make clear the reason for writing this book. There are currently over 28,000 students and more than 1,600 teachers in the fifty-nine schools of the Le Chéile Trust. For everyone involved in the Le Chéile enterprise of education the task of teaching and learning is taking place within a rapidly-changing society where new challenges are being encountered constantly in our school communities. What does the Le Chéile founding story have to say to this situation? What can today's teacher learn from the school's heritage and how can he or she benefit from the legacy of the remarkable founders who shared their gifts so generously with their contemporaries, who in turn handed on this charism from one generation to the next. The answer to these questions lies in the area of spirituality. Our concern is not to promote a sense of nostalgia for a vanishing past but to celebrate a new awareness of how the gifts of the congregations can be lived for today. The key to this lies in exploring the spirituality of teaching and learning that can be gleaned from the founding stories. So having considered the historical contexts in which the founders worked we will go on to suggest ways in which their spirituality can find expression in today's schools and in the lives of the people who are sharing this journey with us.

The founders lived very much in the present and as people of faith they were open to the ways in which the Spirit of God enabled them to live fully engaged with the opportunities and challenges that surrounded them. Our desire is to learn from their openness, courage and generosity so that new generations can benefit from the gifts they shared and so that Le Chéile schools can continue to be witnesses to the belief that 'transformative education is essentially a spiritual process' (*The Le Chéile Charter*). Underpinning this idea is a belief that the Spirit of God continues to gift the Church in its mission of education and that this same Spirit continues to inspire those who seek the wisdom that comes from above. Deriving a living spirituality from the stories of the founders is a vital link in the Le Chéile vision for Catholic education and a process that we wish to promote through this book.

Six of the congregations were founded in France, four were founded in England, one in Italy and three in Ireland.

Historical Context for the Irish Le Chéile Congregations

Irish history, and specifically the history of the Irish Catholic school, is the locus for the founding of three Le Chéile congregations in Ireland and the reason why eleven other congregations, though founded and established elsewhere, moved here to found congregational schools. Looking briefly at the history of their times, the story of each congregation, its founding values and its desire to ensure its distinctive heritage will continue in its schools in the future.

Irish Historical Context – Fifth–Sixteenth century

The historical story begins with St Patrick whose missionary work in the fifth century provides the initial link in the threads of faith and education. The education and faith mission was developed in the middle-ages by the founding of Irish monasteries and their schools. In the year AD 563, St Columba brought the mission to Scotland, and St Aidan established another monastery in Lindisfarne, northern England. The mission continued through the land of the Anglo-Saxon and then to the Frankish Empire (Europe today), Columbanus having gone to Bobbio, Italy, in AD 615. A number of foundations followed in France, Germany, Belgium and Switzerland. In the context of locating the fourteen Le Chéile congregations and their schools we note faith and education spreading and being served by Irish missions to Great Britain and then to mainland Europe in the sixth and seventh centuries. The Le Chéile story will include how English and European congregations would come to Ireland in the service of faith and education in later centuries. The Irish historical threads of mission, learning, schools and connection with Europe were woven in the early centuries and are in the tapestry of the community of schools in the new Trust.

Ireland survived the Viking wars of the ninth and tenth centuries and came to be described as 'the island of saints and scholars' in the eleventh and twelfth centuries. A Le Chéile founder can be connected to this historical period. While twelfth–thirteenth century Ireland was thriving in faith and learning, Dominic, founder of the Dominican family, was confronting heresy in France. His friars came to Ireland in the thirteenth century. It was these men, with Augustinian and Franciscan 'friars beggars' as they were called, who, through their preaching and administration of the sacraments, would keep religion alive during the period of the Tudor Reformation.

The Penal Laws (1691–1778)

The Tudor regime in the sixteenth century and its Reformation legislation were followed by the Penal Law period in the seventeenth and eighteenth centuries. The laws were introduced gradually and were of three kinds:

1. The Catholic hierarchy and regular clergy were outlawed. Secular clergy, if they registered with the government, could remain.

2. Catholics were not allowed to hold official and governance positions or enter certain professions unless they took an oath denying the authority of the papacy and other Catholic doctrines.

3. Catholics were forbidden to hold property.

4. Critically, and of specific interest for our Le Chéile story, the Penal Laws attempted to outlaw the Catholic education system. The Act to prevent the further growth of popery (1704), gave

power to justices of the peace to pursue any family who sent children abroad for education. However Irish Catholics continued to travel secretly to Irish colleges in Europe, and Daniel Delaney, founder of the Patrician Brothers, is an example of how this penal law could be circumvented. Only the Established (Anglican) Church could legally have places of worship, dignified by the name 'church'. The monasteries and churches, which had escaped Tudor confiscation, were taken over by the Anglican Church. The Dominican Sisters were in Galway during these penal times. They survived the Tudor, Cromwellian and penal times, even going into exile for a while. They established a Catholic school for girls despite the difficulties and challenges. Daniel Delaney, founder of the Patrician Brothers was born in penal times, 1747. Margaret Aylward, founder of the Holy Faith Sisters, was born in 1810 when the movement for Catholic emancipation was beginning. The ability of the Roman Catholic population to maintain their faith through the Tudor and Penal centuries would lead to the political demand for full emancipation in the nineteenth century.

CATHOLIC SCHOOL MISSION IN THE NINETEENTH CENTURY

This is the century of post-penal laws, Catholic Emancipation in 1829, famine in the 1840s and a resurgent Catholic church in the second half of the century. This was the century that witnessed the beginning of a new Irish Catholic middle class, a central contextual feature in the Le Chéile congregational founding stories. Evangelical missions supported by English finance had both political and religious motivation. Daniel O'Connell's successful emancipation campaign aroused intense unease among many Protestants. Catholic activists opened schools where children were provided with food and education. St Vincent de Paul societies were formed and, according to one modern historian, Susan Moffitt, the most formidable activist and opponent of the proselytizing mission was Margaret Aylward. Along with the Holy Faith Sisters, Aylward also founded a St Vincent de Paul branch for women in Dublin.

Each of the founding narratives of the three Irish congregations is situated in a particularly fraught period of Irish history and connects with earlier periods of the history of Christianity in

Ireland: the Dominican Sisters of Cabra (1819), claim direct and unbroken links to the Cromwellian period; Daniel Delaney's Brotherhood (1808), to St Patrick as patron, and the Holy Faith Sisters (1867), to the era of nineteenth-century proselytizing and post-famine poverty. The outcomes were the foundation of religious congregations whose members would commit their lives to values with historical origins: the gospel mission, defending the Catholic faith and providing schools for the poor and the developing middle class. Each congregational founder, called by God in a particular time and in a particular place, responded by developing a family of religious members with its own founding narrative and distinctive founding values. We aim to link contextual history, congregational narratives and founding congregational values with the desire of the congregations to ensure that their distinctive heritages would continue in their schools in the future.

In this same nineteenth century access to Catholic secondary education grew for those who could afford it, and by 1870 there were seventy large Catholic secondary schools. These were schools founded, managed and staffed by religious congregations. They were essentially not state or fee-paying schools (run for personal profit or gain), and were laying the foundation for as yet undreamed of opportunities for education in Ireland.

The founding of the three indigenous Irish congregations, the Dominican Sisters (Galway in the seventeenth century and Dublin in the nineteenth), the Patrician Brothers (Carlow in the eighteenth century), and the Holy Faith Sisters (Dublin in the nineteenth century), are the first stories to be explored.

The Irish Dominican Sisters

The Irish Dominican Sisters are members of the Order of Preachers founded by St Dominic in the thirteenth century. Their mission, like his, is to preach the truth of the gospel.

Dominic de Guzmán began his extraordinary mission in 1203 by responding to a royal request to assist in a marriage between the king's son and a Danish princess. Two years later Dominic and his friend, Diego, set out to escort the betrothed princess to Castille. The princess either died on the journey, or decided against the marriage, but Dominic sent word of the failed plans to the king and informed him that he and Diego were travelling to Rome to visit the Pope. It was while travelling through France that Dominic began his dedicated mission for faith and truth. To understand the mission we need to know the man.

Dominic was born in Caleruega, in Old Castille in 1170. His parents, Felix and Jane de Guzmán, were of Spanish nobility, and it is believed that they were related to the reigning house of Castille. Jane d'Aza was renowned for her holiness and was canonised by Pope Leo XII in 1826. At the age of fourteen Dominic left this privileged home to dedicate himself to prayer and study at the University of Palencia remaining there for ten years. Ordained a priest in 1195, he began what he believed would be a monastic and contemplative life. But God had other plans. On a journey to Rome through France with his friend Diego, Dominic witnessed the spiritual damage of the Albigensian heresy whose followers believed that material creation was intrinsically evil. This placed them at odds with the Church which holds that God not only created matter but whose Son, Jesus Christ, was born into the material world. Ironically, at the time of the heresy the Church itself needed its own reform. Travelling through Toulouse, Diego and Dominic witnessed with amazement and sorrow the spiritual ruin wrought by the false teaching and resolved to address it by gathering people who could dedicate themselves to teaching the truth. The Pope asked them to go to Languedoc and work with the Cistercians, to whom he had entrusted a specific mission to address the challenges. Dominic brought a new energy to this mission and encouraged the Cistercians to adopt a more austere way of life. Great numbers of Cistercians reformed, and they lost no time in engaging with Dominic in spirited debate on matters of faith. Whenever an opportunity arose they accepted the opportunity to teach and to challenge. The thorough training that Dominic had received at Palencia proved to be of inestimable value to him in his own encounters and challenges.

Early in his new ministry Dominic thought about developing an institution that would protect women from the influence of false teaching. He noted that many women had been educated in false theories and having embraced them had become active propagandists. They had founded schools in which the children of the Catholic nobility were being educated. To address this Dominic, with the permission of the Bishop of Toulouse, established a convent of women at Prouille in 1206. To this community he gave the rule and constitutions which have ever since guided the women of the Order of St Dominic. What an interesting foundation in the thirteenth century, recognition of the education and critical role of women and a foundation of women before Dominic formally organised his male followers!

By 1214, the influence of Dominic's preaching and the eminent holiness of his life had drawn around him a small band of devoted disciples eager to follow wherever he might lead. Dominic never forgot his aim, first thought of eleven years before, of founding a religious order to combat false teaching and propagate religious truth. This was the beginning of a very public ministry, and he was sowing seeds in the founding of the new Dominican family. It was also the beginning of a new form of religious life, active and involved in the daily lives of ordinary people. Dominic realised that in order to preach and teach there had to be sound study and training. Within the Dominican family of women and men the founding values of faith, truth, and compassion expressed in lives of preaching and teaching were evident. Dominic's first schools were concerned with the truths of the Catholic faith. The origin of the Dominican motto *Veritas* ('truth') is rooted within these original values. Dominic would lead future preachers and teachers in the mission of providing people with an intelligent appreciation of, and formation in, the Catholic faith. Dominic de Guzmán died in 1221.

There were two outstanding figures in the early Dominican story: the thirteenth-century theologian and philosopher, St Thomas Aquinas, Doctor of the Church and patron of colleges and schools, and the fourteenth-century theologian and Doctor of the Church, St Catherine of Siena. Eight hundred years after Thomas Aquinas joined the Order of St Dominic he remains one of the most widely read philosophers and theologians in the world, an intellectual giant who wrote over sixty works which brought together the best contemporary scholarship from Christian, Muslim and Jewish writers as well as the works of Aristotle. Like Dominic he was simply and passionately interested in the truth. His whole life became a search for the truth, a search to understand the world as it is and to live in it fully and well.

The second great Dominican theologian, Catherine, is an example for courageous women. She was fearless in challenging and guiding the institutional Church of her day, always ready to speak the truth whether she was addressing the Pope and his cardinals or political leaders in Europe. She lived at a time when the Church was divided between leadership in Rome and in Avignon, and she challenged Pope Urban VI to resolve the crisis. She addressed the reform of the Church and she also worked for peace among the squabbling secular states in Italy. A deeply holy woman, one of the great medieval mystics, she attracted many followers, and was popular and well known in her lifetime.

Catherine was conferred with the Church's doctoral status and title in 1970, six hundred years after her death, the first woman of the Church to be so honoured. In 2000 she was named one of the patrons of Europe by John Paul II.

Now we move the Dominican story to the Irish foundation of Dominican Sisters. Written evidence of Dominican women's presence in Galway is recorded in 1644, and the Dominican Sisters today claim that it is here in seventeenth-century Galway that their mission of founding schools for girls in Ireland began. Sr Helen O'Dwyer, former leader of the Dominican Sisters and a member of the founding Le Chéile Working Group, proudly told of how six laywomen wanting to bring Dominic's vision and values to education in Galway, sought direction and support from the Dominican Friars. The Galway nuns survived the vicissitudes of the post-Reformation religious persecution and underwent a period of exile in Spain. They were literally living their lives by stealth when they went underground. Returning to Galway and the challenges of Penal Ireland in the late eighteenth century, a few of them left Galway for Dublin in 1717. They lived firstly in Clontarf and then moved to Cabra. By the end of the eighteenth century the Dominican Sisters were running girls' boarding schools in Galway, Dublin, Drogheda and Waterford. By 1808, at the end of one of the most disastrous periods in Irish history, they were financially destitute. The remaining Sisters risked the little they had and borrowed money to buy a property in Cabra, Dublin, in 1819. They were aware that if they were to carry on and develop a mission of Catholic education for young women, drastic measures had to be taken – they went into debt so that they could meet the needs of their time.

Mother Columba Maher, the prioress of the Cabra convent, had four companions, one a novice. They had few resources. Sr Helen develops the Cabra founding story, 'Again very small, again boarders, even when they were in Channel Row. The Sisters were educated women, they were always well educated.' Formal education for girls was not normal at that time, and only for those families who could pay for it. Parallel to the new small Cabra boarding school for girls the Sisters founded a small primary school for poor children, described by Sr Helen as 'a Robin Hood approach'. A significant thread in the Dominican Sisters' story is that though their founding intention was to educate girls of the emerging middle class in boarding schools, and later in secondary day schools, one of their first schools in Dublin was a primary school for the poor because that was what was needed at the time. The early Sisters were well educated women of Anglo-Irish families, and their own family heritage and culture was invested in the creation of the new schools. The prospectus of the first Cabra secondary boarding school reflects both that family background and the societal changes in Catholic Ireland in the nineteenth century. The girls, according to the prospectus, should be made aware of their position in life and they should 'rise in society'; their Cabra education would permit them to take their place 'with propriety, ease and dignity'. The Dominican Sisters had founded a primary school which was needed for the poor in 1819, and again in 1846 they responded generously to an identified need when they founded a school for deaf girls. This was a courageous and generous response to another need of the time and would contribute significantly to the lives of deaf Irish children.

The Irish Dominican Sisters' story, that of enclosed nuns with a strong leaning toward contemplation, rigorous study and teaching in the pursuit of truth and faith, developed further in the late nineteenth and twentieth centuries. The Dominican Sisters were central in the provision of secondary education for an emerging Irish Catholic middle-class population. They were clearly focused on educating girls and enabling them to take their role with confidence in society and in the Church. In collaboration with the Loreto, Ursuline and other religious sisters they also led the movement for tertiary education for young Catholic women in Ireland. It was not until the religious had their secondary schools well developed and had some experience of advancing the cause of higher education that women who had been to Catholic schools emerged to take their part in the public debates of the day. In 1884 the Dominican Sisters opened a centre of university studies for women in Eccles Street, and in 1930 they opened colleges for girls who wished to have careers in the public service or in the business world. The guiding principles for the Dominican Sisters' education mission were that while the secular part of the education conducted by the Sisters was secondary in importance to the religious, it had to be as thorough. They considered it an obligation of justice to prepare students adequately for the places they deserved to occupy in life.

Their innovative mission continued. In 1909 the Dominican Sisters organised and hosted summer courses for other religious sisters engaged in secondary education throughout the country. In 1929 they, at the invitation of the National Department of Education and the Archbishop of Dublin, formed what was known as a 'Nuns' Association of Headmistresses. 'Nuns' were then invited to the Department of Education Office in Dublin to discuss ongoing developments in Irish education. Eventually, and under Dominican leadership, this group of religious women founded the Conference of Convent Secondary Schools (CCSS). This served Catholic secondary schools for girls until the end of the twentieth century when the Association of Management of Catholic Secondary schools inherited the responsibility for all Catholic secondary Schools. A contemporary and pertinent piece of the story is that a Dominican Sister, Brid Roe, led the early consultation and conversation with other religious congregations which would result in the formation of the Le Chéile Catholic Schools Trust in 2010.

The Irish Dominican Sisters (known as the Cabra Dominicans) are a branch of the international Dominican family, composed of women and men, spread throughout the world and dedicated to proclaiming the truth. They consider knowledge in all its forms as truth to be discovered. They see their task as fundamentally a synthesis of faith and culture.

From Prouille in the thirteenth century through Galway in the seventeenth, Dublin in the eighteenth and nineteenth centuries to the Le Chéile Trust in the twenty-first century, Dominic's heritage of faith and truth are lived and reflected through the lives and mission of the Dominican Sisters, their lay-colleagues and school leaders, and the students of their schools. Sr Helen provides the primary Dominican thread for Le Chéile weaving,

Truth is a core value for us Dominicans, and no matter where the Dominicans are today that is their motto, Veritas, so we have kept it and our education is rooted in that value.

That core value is operative in contemporary school life as outlined in the words of Mary Daly, Principal of St Dominic's Secondary School, Ballyfermot: 'We live out the Dominican motto of truth in our school as we strive to respect, acknowledge and understand one another.'

Dominican schools and colleges strive to be communities centred on Christ, and on Gospel values, where all work together, learn to make informed judgements, pray together, and forgive each other.

IN IRELAND DOMINICAN/LE CHÉILE SCHOOLS ARE:

- Dominican College, Griffith Avenue, Dublin
- Dominican College, Wicklow
- Dominican College, Galway
- Dominican College, Muckross Park, Dublin
- St Dominic's Secondary School, Ballyfermot, Dublin
- Scoil Chaitriona, Bothar Moibhi, Dublin
- Sion Hill Dominican College, Blackrock
- St Dominic's College, Cabra, Dublin
- Santa Sabina Dominican College, Sutton, Dublin

THE DOMINICAN SISTERS ALSO ACT AS PARTNER TRUSTEE IN:

- Old Bawn Community School, Tallaght with Co. Dublin VEC and the Dominican Fathers.

THE PATRICIAN BROTHERS

The scene is the main street in Tullow, Co. Carlow. The year is 1777. A handsome young priest, Fr Daniel Delany, is walking along the street and passers by might notice that he is looking dejected and worried. If they stopped and spoke to him he might tell them that he was wondering what possible good he was doing in his parish. He had begun to reflect on all that had brought him to this place. Within this 'reflection' we locate the story of the Patrician Brothers which lies deep within the context of early Patrician Irish history and in the Franco–Irish Catholic educational relationship. An Irish priest/bishop, in the clerical lineage and mission of Patrick, is the founder of the Patrician Brothers.

Daniel Delany was born in Laois in 1747, a time which has been described by some historians as the darkest period of Irish history. Daniel's mother, a widow struggling to maintain a small family farm, sent him to live with her sisters. His aunts provided the rudiments of his early formal learning and, as schooling for Catholics was illegal, they sent him to a local hedge school. A contemporary description of a hedge school tells of a hut built of sods in a ditch, without a door, window or chimney. A hole in the roof of the hut served as a chimney and provided light. Daniel's rudimentary education in the hedge school was supplemented by Latin lessons from the local priest. These learning sessions may have contributed to his priestly vocation. His aunts who had local Protestant friends borrowed Latin books for his studies. For secondary schooling, like all Irish Catholics who could afford it,

Daniel went abroad but secretly as such education was illegal. At the age of seventeen he went to the College des Lombards in Paris in 1764. There he joined a prestigious community of priests and clerical students. He learned a new language and a new culture. The alumni of such a college was remarkable for varied knowledge of the world, and brought to the clerical ministry the manners of cultivated gentlemen. The French College educating emigrant Irish students is an interesting link to the Irish monks who in earlier centuries had journeyed to Europe bringing faith and learning. Daniel and his companions were benefiting from that early mission.

Following his ordination, and after an absence of twelve years, Daniel returned to Ireland. From his French education and his formation in a centre of piety and culture, this young man came home to an uneducated, impoverished people engaged in agrarian and civil unrest. Squalor was the norm. In a statistical and contemporary review of the Irish countryside at this time Sir Charles Coote wrote: 'Of the houses of the people few deserve to be classed better than hovels. The pigs of England have more comfortable dwellings than the majority of the Irish peasantry'. The Cromwellian invasion, agrarian rebellion and the Penal Laws had deepened the problems of an impoverished people. Br Cormac Commins, a Patrician leader and member of the founding Le Chéile Working Group, says 'when he returned he was absolutely appalled at what he saw – drunkenness, faction fighting, this is what he saw when he came to Tullow.' Br Cormac continues 'wakes for example would last for days … It was an orgy of drunkenness, that was the practice in many cases and even the remains were brought from the house to the cemetery, there was no such thing as going to the church.' He offers an explanation for this behaviour: 'I suppose one reaction to injustice is anarchy … if the only laws they know were penal or anti-human that is reaction to it. The people were de-humanised by the laws or by the injustice, and that is the way they reacted.'

The lack of even a basic education or a modicum of faith depressed him so much that he was tempted to return to France. However, his mother persuaded him to remain, and his uncle, also a priest, reminded him that it was for the impoverished Irish he had been ordained. With this advice and his mother's persuasion Daniel responded generously and was assigned to the parish of Tullow, Co. Carlow. Thus an ardent, cultivated and eloquent young priest began his Irish ministry. Each Sunday – to the few who attended – he preached against the abuses of intolerance, injustice, excessive drinking, and faction fighting. His eloquent preaching was entertaining but not effective. The behaviours of the people reflected the awful circumstances in which they lived, and his words, however eloquent, were not going to change them. Daniel adopted another tactic. He continued to preach on Sunday, but he also began to walk the country roads and visit the homes. He then included visits to the venues of gaming and fighting, speaking to and disbanding the groups. When these were dispersed they just gathered elsewhere, and he became increasingly discouraged.

A special moment was critical in the development of Daniel's mission. On his way home one evening, tired, dispirited and worrying what to do, Daniel came upon a group of children playing and singing on a mud-patch in the town. He always stopped to speak to children, and though very weary once more, he stopped as usual and listened to their song. They were singing a verse of the *Ave Maris Stella* from the Vespers of Our Lady as they played their games. They only knew one verse, in half Latin, half English. A vesper hymn in the play of impoverished Irish children became the seed for an important mission. Daniel invited the children to come to the Chapel on Sunday and learn more hymns. They came in increasing numbers and Daniel taught them simple melodies, sacred and secular with and without words. The language of the hymn was not a barrier, Latin, French or English, the children loved them and sang them all with equal enjoyment. After each singing lesson Daniel also taught them about God. He related his words to what they had been singing, or to something already learned, or to some matter of daily concern. Then they would pray together. These were lessons without books. The children could not read and there were no books. A choir was formed, and Daniel's mother made surplices for them to wear. They sang each Sunday at Mass. A band developed, and the 'ha'penny whistle' became a badge of honour. Br Cormac explained:

He (Daniel) felt he had failed to get adults to respond to his teaching, his preaching ... so he felt he would concentrate his efforts on the young people, and that was the origin of it, and that is how we find ourselves in education today ... there were literally no schools and our beloved founder saw education as a way of remedying some of the problems.

Parents and other adults began to attend Mass on Sunday and within the year singers and non-singers were receiving religious instruction. Volunteers were recruited to assist with the teaching. Daniel Delany's Sunday school sessions were the founding of the Patrician mission in faith and education and was the forerunner of their schools. Systematic training of the volunteer instructors was critical. They were formed firstly in their own spirituality, in a deep love of, and faith in God, and they were to be instructors not just in catechism but in the reforming of behaviour so that the children would receive the example of good Christian lives. Raising morale, and improving the lives of the people through faith development and education, became the Patrician Brothers' mission. In 1783 Daniel was consecrated bishop and continued to direct the formation and training of those who were teaching in his Sunday schools. Every journey to visit his people in the diocese entailed travelling that was both difficult and dangerous. Biased officials, legal discrimination, violence, poverty, fear, ignorance and drunkenness were companions on each lonely journey. Clergy were living in fear and chapels were on the point of collapse. Then in 1798 Daniel's diocese was directly involved in a political rebellion. A priest-leader, Fr Murphy was executed in Tullow and his Catholic chapel confiscated for military use. People lived in terror. Daniel Delany renewed his pre-rebellion plans and quietly continued to minister to those who were open to his love and gentleness. He wished to provide more permanence to his work and so he decided to establish communities of men and women who would devote their lives to the gospel mission of faith and education.

Bishop Daniel Delany was now sixty years of age, but his work was not done. In fact, it was in the phase of a new beginning. Like Dominic, centuries before, Daniel organised a religious congregation of women in the first instance. He invited six women from his confraternity of trained catechists to form the first post-Reformation community to be called the Sisterhood of St Brigid, now know as the Brigidine Sisters. This founding was on the feast of St Brigid, 1 February 1807. A year and a day later, on 2 February 1808, he invited four men into the parish chapel in Tullow, and established the Brothers of St Patrick, the Patrician Brothers. James Mc Mahon, a strolling scholar and hedge school-master living far from home, and local labourers, Ambrose Dawson, Richard Fitzpatrick and Maurice Cummins were the first Brothers and their monastery was Daniel's little ramshackle chapel. The chief duty of the new community was to instruct the poor, and on Sundays they provided religious instruction to the children of the parish in the Chapel. Br Mc Mahon continued to teach, and the other founding Brothers laboured to provide for their companion in mission. The Brothers' first school house, built by themselves, was a thatched house built of stone and mud and costing about £10.

When Daniel Delany died in 1814, the new community continued to found monasteries and schools, moving to Galway, Fethard and Mallow. Br Cormac speaks about the Patrician Brothers' significant involvement in Galway during famine times. They ran a system called the 'Breakfast Institute' for the poor. One of the early Brothers, Paul O'Connor, had walked from Tullow to Galway to work with those who were living in famine destitution.

This congregation of religious men which was founded by Bishop Daniel Delany was to experience many difficulties and challenges after his death, but foundations in Ireland and abroad continued. Each new beginning reflected Daniel Delaney's founding intention of providing schools for children, providing them with an education which would fit them for life and would nurture their faith.

Daniel Delany's story, and the values which influenced the early development of the Patrician Brothers and their schools, are now rich threads within the inheritance tapestry of the Le Chéile Catholic Schools Trust. Michael Stacey, a former Principal of Patrician College, Finglas, reflects Daniel Delany's values as lived today, the children that we have, they are coming to school with all their diverse talents and characteristics and what we have got to make sure of is that when they leave school, that their characteristic is a Christian one. We want them to treat people with respect, and that when they see hurt being done that they can actually step in and be able to say 'that's wrong'.

In their schools the Brothers aim to recognise a variety of needs among students ... and they value a close working rapport with the partners who share their commitment to education. Foremost among those partners are their working colleagues in the schools, the parents of the students and the leaders of the local church.

IN IRELAND PATRICIAN / LE CHÉILE SCHOOLS ARE:

- Patrician College, Finglas, Dublin
- Patrician Presentation, Fethard, Co. Tipperary
- Patrician Secondary School, Newbridge, Co. Kildare
- St Joseph's College, Galway

THE PATRICIAN BROTHERS ALSO ACT AS PARTNER TRUSTEE IN:

- Tullow Community School, Co. Carlow (with Brigidine Sisters and Carlow VEC)
- Mountrath Community School, Co. Laois (with Brigidine Sisters and Laois VEC)

THE HOLY FAITH SISTERS

*A nineteenth-century dark, miserable Dublin prison cell is the scene for
the birth of the third Le Chéile Irish religious congregation. The impulse
to found the Holy Faith Sisters and schools was born in the mind of a
Waterford woman while she was in prison.*

The story begins with Margaret Aylward in the women's prison in
Dublin in 1860. She is fifty years old and in very poor health. In
November of that year she was sentenced by the Court of the
Queen's Bench to six months imprisonment, and ordered to pay all
legal costs. The controversial case, which concerned the fosterage
placement of an infant girl, had been closely followed on both sides
of the Irish Sea, and provided the media with drama and debate
throughout Margaret's court case and the six-month sentence. The
incarceration in a common jail of a prominent lady of high social
standing, following on the dismissal of the original charge against
her of kidnapping, was in itself of media interest, but the added
interests of a major Church/State dispute, and claims of collusion
between the prosecuting party and a prominent English evangelical
society, not to mention the questions surrounding the fitness of the
judge to officiate, provided unrelenting and fascinating media
material. The charge on which she was found guilty was contempt
of court because she could not give the address of the fostering
family in which the child in question had been placed. The family
had actually left Ireland. The fact that Margaret was interred with

convicted prisoners resulted in sensational editorials in all the major newspapers, including the *London Times*. The newly-formed *Irish Times* was merciless in its attack on the 'semi-nun', so-called because of her sober dress. The *Dublin Morning News* defended her, seeing her incarceration as an attack on the rights of Catholics and depicting her as a martyr. Support from bishops, religious and laypeople in Ireland and England failed to prevent her imprisonment. Archbishop Dixon of Armagh visited Rome and reported the circumstances of Margaret's case to Pope Pius IX, he there and then sent Margaret his blessing and a cameo of the Mother of Sorrows. Public subscription lists were opened to defray her legal expenses. Cardinal Cullen, the first Irish Cardinal drove in a horse-drawn carriage to visit her in prison, and this drew further ire from the *London Times* 'Dr Cullen, the athletic Catholic white-washer, advances, in confident conviction of Protestant gullibility to call down the sympathy of the world for the poor prisoner, Margaret Aylward.' On the 5 May 1861, her sentence completed to the very day, she left prison at 6am and walked to Arran Quay to attend Mass. Margaret was fifty-one years of age. She returned to Eccles Street, the centre of her mission. There were significant outcomes from her time spent in prison, including her deteriorating health and the fact that her lay-companions had dispersed. Now her mind was focused on the need to begin a religious congregation of stable membership to serve her mission and staff her schools. Thus was born the Holy Faith Sisters and their schools.

Margaret had been born into a Catholic merchant community in Waterford in 1810. This community has been described as a community of families confident in themselves, of some wealth and therefore of some education. Margaret's was one of the most prominent families; she was one of ten children. Her mother was substantially wealthy in her own right, her father a successful trader, so Margaret was in touch with business from an early age. An attractive, strong young woman she developed exceptional business skills, and had an excellent command of language. Political issues were normal in the family conversations, and visitors to the Aylward home included Daniel O'Connell, the Liberator, Thomas Francis Meagher, a Young Irelander, and Edmund Rice, Founder of the Christian Brothers. As befitted their status the Aylwards sent their children to the best Catholic schools available in Ireland and England. Margaret went to the Ursulines in Thurles, her sister to the Benedictines in England, and her brothers went to the Jesuit Colleges, Clongowes and Stonyhurst. Margaret's Ursuline learning included fluent French, Art, Latin and, interestingly, Irish heritage and culture. Margaret's family was connected to the Christian Brothers, her uncle being one of the first companions of Edmund Rice. A lifelong regard for the Brothers and their mission would influence her schools, especially their provision of family relief and tuition for poor Waterford boys and the provision of Irish textbooks for Irish children. She also had direct links, again through her mother's family, with the Presentation Sisters. After leaving school she worked as a volunteer lay-teacher in their schools. She twice entered religious life, the Ursulines and, later, the Sisters of Charity, but on each occasion she found the loss of liberty and health difficulties too great a strain. Her intention then was to serve the mission of Jesus Christ as a laywoman. Believing that there might be criticism of her religious life failures, she moved to Dublin.

Margaret lived first with her brother John in Clontarf, and then moved to Gardiner Street to be closer to the source of her mission, the poor. This move initiated her life-long involvement with Dublin's slums and poor. The Dublin of 1848 was a city of contrasts. There were terraces of stately town houses, gracious malls and grand squares but behind these were warrens of mud hovels and sheds. Housing for the poor was appalling and rents exorbitant. The city in 1845–7 was a refuge for the dispossessed and most destitute, with some leaving for what they believed would be a new life in England, America or Australia. Dublin's slums were packed with women and children, widowed, orphaned and abandoned, or left behind as their menfolk sought work abroad. Margaret Aylward began by visiting these women and children, not just to provide material relief but also to listen to them. She gathered companions to make these visits with her, the sisters, daughters and wives of middle-class and wealthy Dublin men. In training her helpers she repeatedly stressed the role and dignity of each poor person. The visitors' counsel and care were the principal end of their ministry, insisting that attentive and respectful listening were as important as the pecuniary and material relief which they brought. Margaret saw this as the way to cherish Christ in each who shared in 'the dignity of children of God'. Providing for the immediate material needs of the poor was met side-by-side with a conscious ministry of fostering self-respect and confidence in themselves and in a loving God.

Affectionately known to the Dublin slum-dwellers as 'the lady Aylward' she was described by a contemporary as one 'of great and noble mind'. She founded the Ladies' Association of Charity, a powerful organisation of socially committed women which she introduced to the city of Dublin. It was the first Dublin branch of St Vincent de Paul. The work of St Brigid's Orphanage, a boarded-out or family system of foster care was her next initiative. Orphan children were received in St Brigid's in Eccles Street, and were then fostered into caring Catholic families. She was strongly opposed to institutional orphanages for children, and support for family life was a key value in all her work. St Brigid's boarding-out Orphanage was innovative and attracted even the attention of speakers in the British House of Commons. In all her mission endeavours she was partnered, guided and supported by the saintly Fr John Gowan, a Vincentian priest.

Margaret spoke publicly of, and exposed, the evils of poverty. She addressed injustice and inspired others to follow her example. Visiting the poor had alerted her to the dangers of proselytism. In a more ecumenical age we do not experience such activities, but Margaret was very exercised by her experience of the Evangelical Church Missions and their work among the poor to wean them from their Catholic Faith. She found that poor mothers and children were especially vulnerable to loss of their faith and she was going to defend them. For the rest of her life she was to be identified in a leadership role defending the faith of children especially the children of the poor. This was the controversial work which led indirectly to her imprisonment. It also led to her founding, in late middle age, a new religious congregation, the Sisters of the Holy

Faith. As a fearless woman campaigner she made a major impact on the Ireland of her day in the areas of child-care, education of the poor, religious life and centrally, the defence of the faith.

Faith was the core value in Margaret Aylward's every decision. Within five months of her release from prison in 1861 this tireless woman, with Fr Gowan's support, founded her first Catholic School of St Brigid. She said: 'Upon this one thing, the education of the poor, depends the future of Ireland and the future of society'. It became evident that both the families and the mission of defending the faith needed schools. Sr Margo Delaney, a Holy Faith congregational leader believes that:

> when she was in prison the notion of the schools became clear …
> her starting point was not society as such, it was the individual, but
> if she could uplift the dignity and give the skills of life to an
> individual poor Catholic child, she felt she was creating a better
> society.

St Brigid was chosen as patron for the orphanage and for the primary schools. One of Margaret's earliest biographers, Margaret Gibbons, tells us that it was Fr Gowan, who suggested St Brigid as the Holy Faith patron. During his missionary time abroad he had heard poor immigrant Irish women called 'Irish Biddies', and he made a resolution that he would make the name of Brigid honoured.

Holy Faith secondary schools were to follow the founding of primary schools. Explicit mention is made of fee-paying schools in the request for congregational status made by Margaret Aylward to Cardinal Cullen in 1866. Hearing that many farmers and middle class Catholics wanted an Irish Catholic secondary education for their daughters the Holy Faith Sisters opened a boarding school in Glasnevin in 1873. Sr Margo explains:

> Cardinal Cullen alerted her to the lack of facilities for young women
> of middle class Catholic parents … so it was not a big jump for her
> to say, 'well, we have educated to this level now, and if the cardinal
> wants this, it is the will of God'.

Margaret Aylward herself wrote that the principal object of these schools would be the faith, claiming that the children attending Holy Faith schools would be educated to be strong in faith – 'a faith that is living and operative'. Deirdre Gogarty, principal of Holy Faith Secondary School, Clontarf, explains a core traditional Holy Faith value in the contemporary school: 'I think that active faith and compassion, the love of the poor and the willingness to act, I think that is very strong ... the hands on approach to Christianity.'

A significant key value for Margaret Aylward was the value of the lay-vocation. This value is evident in all the choices she made in her service of the Faith. She founded a lay-group, she intended it to remain a lay-group, and she formed and directed it as a lay group. When St Brigid's Orphanage Association was formed in the winter of 1856, Margaret set about putting into operation her long-thought-of scheme of a 'House of Rest' where those ladies who were free to do so, might live in prayer and recollection when not engaged in the active services of their Association. Founding a religious congregation was a second choice.

Margaret died in 1878. Her heritage includes: a passionate and courageous commitment to the preservation of, and education in, the Catholic faith, an active compassion and respect for the poor, emphasis on the dignity of each person, the central role of family, and a clear recognition of the lay vocation in the Church's mission. The Sisters of the Holy Faith contribute these coloured threads to the Le Chéile Trust's emerging tapestry of collaborative con-gregational schools.

Holy Faith mission is rooted in a profound appreciation of the gift of faith which has been received from Margaret Aylward who said:

And, indeed, it is a glorious thing to devote our time, talents and energies to the preservation of the faith.

IN IRELAND HOLY FAITH/LE CHÉILE SCHOOLS ARE:

- Holy Faith Secondary School, Clontarf, Dublin
- St David's Holy Faith Secondary School, Greystones, Co. Wicklow
- St Mary's Secondary School, Glasnevin, Dublin
- St Mary's Secondary School, Killester, Dublin
- St Michael's Secondary School, Finglas, Dublin

THE HOLY FAITH SISTERS ALSO ACT AS PARTNER TRUSTEE IN:

- St Wolstan's Community School, Celbridge, Co. Kildare (with Archdiocese of Dublin and Kildare VEC)
- Tallaght Community School, Dublin (with Marist Brothers and County Dublin VEC)

HISTORICAL CONTEXT FOR THE ENGLISH LE CHÉILE CONGREGATIONS

The founding stories of the Society of the Holy Child Jesus, the Sisters of St Paul the Apostle, the Cross and Passion Sisters, and the Poor Servants of the Mother of God are located in the history of the English Catholic Church from the sixteenth century Reformation to the nineteenth Century Catholic Relief Acts. History enables us to identify how the words 'Roman Catholicism', 'Protestantism' and 'Anglicanism' came into the English language. Prior to the Reformation the word 'Christian' covered all believers in Jesus Christ. Then Martin Luther came into the story. He was a conscientious German Augustinian monk who wanted to reform the Christian Church. He did not set out to start a revolution but the authorities perceived his actions as revolutionary, communications and negotiations being difficult then, and he was excommunicated in 1521. His followers protested and developed an alternative 'Protestant' Church. John Calvin's Reformed Protestantism later developed in Geneva, and the English Reformation had its own unique development in the royal, personal and political needs of Henry VIII. Political independence from Rome was a salient factor in these developments too.

Political considerations and politically influenced religious zeal led to the English Penal Enactments which are the background for the Le Chéile congregational foundings. Surviving English Catholics (seventeenth to eighteenth centuries) can be gathered into three main groups: the small number of gentry who remained loyal to Roman Catholicism, and who resisted the State Established Church of England; some urban Catholics who managed to gather in towns for Mass, and who sheltered priests; itinerant priests and vagrant Catholics was another recognised category. Being able to connect with the priest was a critical factor in strengthening the attachment to the 'old religion'. Even within the context of an ongoing and vigorous penal priest-hunt. Many were able to evade capture for years. The lives of three notable saints of this period in English history testify to this. St John Wall worked in Worcestershire for twenty-three years, St John Kemble was an active though 'underground' priest in Herefordshire for fifty-four years, and St David Lewis served the Catholics in South Wales for some thirty years.

Each wave of penal laws decreased the numbers of the Catholic population. Parallel to this same decrease in numbers was the depth of resistance and of faith in the surviving English Catholic community. Parallel to the Irish Penal history the English Catholics founded a number of monasteries and convents in mainland Europe. The English College in Rome was reestablished. Because bishops could not operate without taking an Oath of Allegiance to the English monarch, Rome appointed Vicars Apostolic during the reign of James II, and thereafter until the restoration of the Catholic hierarchy in 1850. The Vicars could rarely meet so they conducted their own internal correspondence and how they communicated with Rome. The Vicars used code words. The Pope was 'Mr. Abraham', Rome was called 'Hilton', and Queen Anne referred to as 'Mrs Hobbs'. More seriously, Mass was 'high prayers' and going to confession was being 'at duty'.

Prior to the Relief Acts of 1778, 1791 and 1829, English Catholics were virtually powerless in their own land. There were no Catholic representatives in either of the Houses of Parliament. A few Catholic schools operated in hiding. Some small relief for Catholics was legalised when the English government recognised that it couldn't continue in the 1775 American War of Independence and, at the same time, engage with wars in France and Spain without enlisting the help of Scottish Highlanders. Most of these were

Catholics who would not take the Oath of Allegiance to the English king. Chinks continued to appear in the hard-line English attitude. Relief Acts followed and Catholics could once again be property owners. They began to build churches and schools. After the Catholic Emancipation Act of 1829 they could enter Parliament. Exiled monks and nuns returned, and Irish Catholics leaving their famine-stricken land colonised the reviving English Church. The immigrant Irish brought their own version of devotional Catholicism to the reviving English Catholic Church. Nineteenth-century England witnessed rapid progress in the building of Catholic schools and churches and the founding of religious congregations. There were a few wealthy benefactors but it was mainly the faith and money of poor Catholics that supported the emergence of a renewed Church.

A small group of Cambridge and Oxford University alumni provided another impetus to a renewing English Catholic Church in the nineteenth century. This group included an Anglican clergyman, George Spencer, who while visiting Rome, met Dominic Barberi, an Italian Passionist priest. This meeting would lead to three significant events, Spencer's conversion to Catholicism, Barberi's coming to England and the founding of the Cross and Passion Sisters. Moreover, Spencer was also involved in advising Nicholas Wiseman, the young rector of the English College, to return to the renewing English Catholic Church. This learned young priest would bring, Spencer believed, a certain kudos to the renewing English Catholic Church, and be able to argue competently with Protestant apologists and defenders of the new religion. In 1850 Wiseman became the first English Cardinal in three centuries. He arrived in England to a 'storm of vilification'. The Prime Minister Lord John Russell led the storm. He had the influential and inflammatory support of *The Times*, and, in due course, the Pope and Wiseman were burned in effigy. In Protestant England the appointment of Wiseman was strongly denounced as yet another Roman Catholic encroachment on the rights of the Established Church and of the civil authority. The Oxford Movement in the mid-nineteenth century provided further intellectual momentum within Catholicism. Its aim was to revive elements of Catholic theology and ritual within the Church of England. Many of those involved later converted to the Catholic Church. Their principal intellectual leader was Blessed John Henry Newman.

Leadership of the English Catholic Church in the nineteenth century was divided between Wiseman and Manning (appointed Cardinal in 1865). They effectively led a reviving Catholic Church and were especially keen to provide adequate schooling for the poor, many of whom were immigrant Irish. Cardinal Manning once wryly remarked that he had 'given up working for the people of England, to work for the Irish occupation of England'.

THE SOCIETY OF THE HOLY CHILD JESUS

An energetic and attractive American woman, the wife of a former Episcopalian priest and the mother of five children, seems an unlikely founder for a congregation of religious women in nineteenth century England. The founding of the Society of the Holy Child Jesus was costly – for Cornelia Connelly herself, for her children and even for her husband, whose decision to become a priest in the Catholic Church set the whole process in motion. Cornelia always said the Society was founded 'on a breaking heart'.

Cornelia was born in 1809, the youngest child in a prosperous Philadelphia family, but by the time she was thirteen both her parents had died. From then on she lived with her eldest half-sister and, through her, met and subsequently married a young curate, Pierce Connelly. After their marriage, Pierce accepted responsibility for the Episcopalian church in Natchez, Mississippi. Here their first two children were born and here, too, Pierce, influenced by meetings with a French naturalist, decided to convert to Catholicism. Cornelia followed her husband in this decision. The couple with their children travelled to Rome where they were well received by the English speaking community and by the hierarchy. Even at this early stage, Pierce was exploring the possibility of priesthood within the Catholic church. Such a decision would inevitably involve separation from Cornelia and the break up of their family. The Connellys thought long and hard and prayed earnestly about the matter, and nine years later, in 1844, they finally agreed that he should take this step. Cornelia had to take a solemn vow of chastity before Pierce could begin his training. She consequently looked towards life as a religious and entered the Sacred Heart convent at the Trinita dei Monte. Her faith was being tested and God's plans were slowly emerging.

When Pierce was ordained in 1846 she left the convent in Rome and brought her children to England. There Bishop Wiseman invited her to work in the mission of providing Catholic education for girls. Her abilities were recognised by the English Catholic Church leader who was in the challenging role of leading and re-establishing Catholicism in England after centuries of penal legislation. Cornelia agreed, travelling to Derby where with a few companions she began organising schools for the poor, holding day and night classes and also Sunday classes to accommodate young factory workers. Cornelia told her companions that her soul had 'almost dwelt in hell', and that the new mission was 'founded on a breaking heart'.

The Society of the Holy Child Jesus was begun. The beginning was small and there were many deprivations, but a spirit of peace prevailed. Cornelia was able to inspire in her companions something of the serenity which she had gained in adversity. Teaching was now her mission and purpose, and within this multi-threaded founding story an international mission for Catholic education was begun in England.

Cornelia was both a religious and a business woman in touch with the contemporary world, she was committed to providing a congregation with educated Catholic women. A clear philosophy, with systematic training of teachers, was woven into the founding of the new Society. Sr Carmel Murtagh, a congregational leader talks about these beginnings and stresses that Cornelia had a vision for her schools: 'She had a vision of education across all sectors. Sisters worked in the poorer and parish schools and there were also schools set up to provide an education within a boarding fee-paying setting.'

In Cornelia's lifetime schools were opened in England, France and in the United States. At the request of prominent English Catholics Cornelia formally requested Pope Gregory XVI's permission to found a congregation whose main work would be the Catholic education of girls.

Cornelia's extraordinary marital difficulties continued. Pierce Connelly grew dissatisfied with his new Catholic chaplaincy role and in 1848 he took refuge in Surrey with Henry Drummond the Scottish evangelical polemicist. Pierce claimed total control of the Connelly children. From 1849 to 1858 he pursued a legal process to reassert his conjugal rights. The case was international news. The press depicted Cornelia as 'a cold, cruel-hearted woman and an unnatural mother'. But she refused to give in. The once-submissive wife was now a religious with an iron will who fought her ex-husband priest in court. A court case followed by an appeal ended with Cornelia paying for Pierce's debts. Cornelia always loved him.

The stress experienced by Cornelia was increased by the fact that the Catholic clergy, though approving and sanctioning her new religious congregation and its mission, continued to refer to her as Mrs Connelly. Her greatest suffering, however, was separation from her children. But the mission of the Society of the Holy Child Jesus continued, and Cornelia's faith, strength and reliance on God shaped the spirituality of the new congregation. Love for her children and her experiences of joy and loss in rearing them may have led to her firm devotion to and interest in the theology of the childhood of Jesus. She was fascinated by the realisation that Jesus went through each of the years and processes of childhood. For this reason Cornelia Connelly decided to call her congregation Society of the Holy Child Jesus. Sr Carmel developed this point: 'Incarnation is at the heart of our Congregation, and that is what inspired, and continues to inspire us in education. The person fully alive.'

For the Le Chéile Schools Trust the story continues a century later in Ireland. The Society of the Holy Child came to Ireland nearly a century after the original foundation. Large numbers of Irish girls had been educated in Holy Child schools in England, and many of these students joined the congregation. Educated Irish women also availed of teacher training with the sisters in Preston, England. The Irish-born Sisters were amongst the first groups sent to both the United States and Africa to found new Catholic schools. Ireland in the early twentieth century was fertile ground for vocations to the religious life and this factor influenced the Holy Child Sisters in establishing a community in Ireland for the reception of Irish entrants to the congregation. It is interesting that in 1935 when the congregational leader, Mother Amadeus, was moving this initiative, she explicitly expressed concern that there should be sensitivity about seeing things 'from an Irish point of view', helping Irish entrants and 'not commenting on their brogues'. The Irish faith and commitment outweighed the brogue!

John Charles McQuaid, Archbishop of Dublin (1940–72), figures prominently in the story of the Society's eventual foundation in Killiney, Co. Dublin. Like the nineteenth-century English hierarchy he wanted Catholic fee-paying schools in his diocese as well as schools which were serving the poor. The indigenous Irish congregations, Christian Brothers, Mercy, Presentation and Holy Faith Sisters were already providing schools for the poor and middle class but the growing business and professional classes of Catholics still needed schools. The Society of the Holy Child Jesus accepted the Dublin archdiocesan invitation and on 1 January 1947 there was a formal opening with Mass celebrated in Killiney by Archbishop McQuaid himself. He then entertained the Sisters to breakfast at his own home.

Later in the century the Sisters would be responsible for a community school. Sr Carmel explains:

> We have two schools, one that is a fee-paying secondary school, and the other that is a community school. We are still committed to that vision of education, that offers opportunities to students, that values the person, wants to develop a spirit of enquiry and we believe that the philosophy of education that is our heritage, still has something to offer.

Eileen Morris, a former principal of Holy Child Community School, Sallynoggin, reflects Sr Carmel's belief:

> I have to say that the values of the Holy Child ethos are firmly entrenched in the Holy Child Community School. And this is evident in our interactions with the students … Cornelia Connelly's philosophy, the values of respect and dignity.

As mentioned in the narrative above, the name Society of the Holy Child Jesus (SHCJ) was influenced by Cornelia's maternal role and experience. She was drawn to the childhood of Jesus, the years when He grew 'in age and wisdom and grace'. She was fascinated that God-made-man grew through all the stages of childhood just like us. In her many roles in life: wife, mother, religious founder and teacher, Cornelia Connelly passed on a unique heritage to the Le Chéile Catholic Schools Trust.

Holy Child Sisters serve as members of one international body animated by a common spirit and committed to living the gospel of Jesus Christ.

IN IRELAND HOLY CHILD SISTERS/ LE CHÉILE SCHOOLS ARE:

- Holy Child Secondary School, Killiney, Dublin.
- Holy Child Sisters are the sole trustee of Holy Child Community School, Sallynoggin, Co. Dublin.

THE SISTERS OF CHARITY OF
ST PAUL THE APOSTLE

'Grow your own vocations', wrote St Vincent de Paul to Pere Chauvet of the diocese of Chartres, France in 1645. Pere Chauvet who was living and working in the plague torn Beauce area of southern France had heard about the work of the Sisters of Charity founded by Vincent de Paul. He had written requesting that some of the sisters would come to work with him. Duly admonished by Vincent, Pere Chauvet did grow his own vocations. With the assistance of dedicated aristocratic women he founded the Sisters of St Paul of Chartres.

Sr Phyllis Brady, a congregational archivist, tells the original French founding story:

We go back to the Sisters of St Paul of Chartres in France, because our foundress in England was a member of that congregation. We are three hundred years old, set up in 1696 in the Beauce area, which at that time was ravaged by plague and war. This was about the same time as Vincent de Paul started his mission in Paris.

Pere Chauvet gathered a group of aristocratic women, gave them a small house and they began to teach poor children. Teaching and visiting the poor families became the mission in the French founding of the sisters. The bishop of the diocese gave them his own name, Paul, and St Paul the Great Teacher is the acknowledged patron of the sisters. The French Revolution in 1789 virtually wiped out the congregation. Some sisters went into hiding and emerged again in the Napoleonic era. Napoleon insisted that religious congregations reviving and regrouping must carry the name 'Charity'. Thus began the Sisters of Charity of St Paul the Apostle. Their mission was to the poor, visiting families in their homes and providing schools for their children. This is the remote French context for the English congregation, the Sisters of Charity of St Paul the Apostle, and in the post-Revolution era the congregation spread all over the world and especially in French colonies.

Two hundred years later, and in England, another parish priest needed religious sisters to teach and minister to the poor in Banbury, Oxfordshire, England. Like Pere Chauvet in the seventeenth century he wrote to the Bishop of Chartres, and was supported in his request by Bishop Wiseman. Sr Phyllis narrates:

> Fr Tandy was parish priest in Banbury, it was a dissolute place, total poverty, and he was like Pere Chauvet, he saw the poor children hungry and needing education. A member of his parish had been to Chartres and was going to enter the convent there and told him about the sisters. So Fr Tandy, with the blessing of his bishop, went to Chartres and asked for sisters.

He was not told 'to grow his own vocations'. The response came in the person of Sr Genevieve Dupuis, a religious sister of St Paul of Chartres.

Genevieve was born in 1813 into post-Revolutionary France. Her home sheltered priests and Genevieve and her siblings received both academic and religious education from these priests. 'It is to them I owe my vocation', she used to say to the sisters when she joined the congregation of St Paul at Chartres in 1834. This congregation was a typical example of the many new French religious congregations emerging in the seventeenth century. The Chartres Sisters saw themselves primarily as servants of their diocese, devoted to the education of poor children, nursing and social work. The bishop was the congregational general leader but the sisters were directed by his clerical nominee. The sisters had survived exile or had worked underground during the French

Revolution, so when the request came from Fr Tandy for sisters to come to England, the bishop, acting as congregational leader, told Genevieve to set out for England and she obeyed. In 1847 Genevieve Dupuis and one companion sailed for England to begin a new chapter in the congregation's story, the founding of an English community. She was to be known as Mother Dupuis, and took charge of Fr Tandy's school in Banbury. She is described as a wise and courageous woman, known for her great faith, hard work and personal charm. She came because she was sent on mission. Genevieve Dupuis had poor English and she and her companion had to dress in lay-clothes because of the anti-Catholic culture in England at that time. She endeavoured to continue her close relationship with the Mother House in Chartres, visiting that community each year. In 1864 the new English congregation received official approval, and Selly Park in Birmingham became the Mother House.

Mother Dupuis and the sisters in Chartres believed that they were just expanding the congregation and providing England with religious sisters of St Paul of Chartres. They intended to maintain normal links with the Mother House in France. Bishop Ullathorne decided that the community at Banbury, and its growing number of branch houses, would be directly under his jurisdiction. Thus it became an English congregation, forced to break off from its French origin. The umbilical link which had connected the sisters to their Mother House was officially cut. This must have been a very painful separation for Genevieve Dupuis and the French sisters but they carried with them the charism of love for poor through home visitation, Catholic schools and service to the parish. Sr Phyllis spoke reverently of the early sisters: 'In England we were parish sisters really. We lived like part of a parish. The parish was our family. We went to weddings and we did the altar and we went to funerals.'

From Chartres, through Banbury, the sisters came to Ireland. This is the next chapter in their story. They arrived in 1903, the year Mother Dupuis died. The connection this time was through the bishop of Limerick who had two sisters in the English community. Sr Phyllis explains:

Bishop Dwyer of Limerick invited them to Kilfinane where there was a primary school. The first sisters lived in a house known as the Priory at the end of the town ... and the parish priest and people of Kilfinane collected money to build a convent.

Kilfinane, Co. Limerick, would have been considered remote in that time and the girls of the town and area had no opportunity to attend secondary school. The sisters took them in as boarders in the convent, or they lodged in the town and thus the sisters provided the first secondary school for Kilfinane in 1926.

Majella Deasy, school principal in Greenhills, Dublin, reflecting on the values in the founding story claimed:

> I would see all of those values in the school, but to different degrees. And in relation to faith, I can clearly recognise that in the Sisters who are present in the schools, because although we have three Sisters who are retired, they are here every day, and I think that that still lives through them very much, in our ethos. ... Last year was the year of St Paul, so we had a very big celebration of that, we had a Mass for the whole school, and a lot of preparation, a lot of thought and a lot of planning. We did our very best to encourage the girls to be involved, and to appreciate their heritage and I try on public occasions to bring St Paul the 'Great Teacher' into what I am doing.

St Paul's Christian faith and teaching from Damascus in the first century, through Chartres in the seventeenth, Banbury in the nineteenth and to Kilfinane, Ireland in the twentieth is a faith heritage which travelled well thanks to Pere Chavet, Fr Tandy and Mother Dupuis and her Sisters.

The world of Paul is little different from ours. We experience the same war and peace, greed and generosity, bravery and cowardice. Although his letters were to the Churches he founded, his message is applicable to us today. He puts before us the fact that God has sent the Spirit of his Son into our hearts so we can say 'Abba, Father' in the secure knowledge that we are the sons and daughters of God.

In Ireland Sisters of Charity of St Paul the Apostle /
Le Chéile schools are:

- Scoil Pól, Kilfinane, Co. Limerick
- St Paul's Secondary School, Greenhills, Dublin

THE SISTERS OF THE CROSS AND PASSION

Attending Mass in Stone's Crown Inn, a Staffordshire English pub, and listening to an Italian Passionist priest so affected Elizabeth Prout that she converted from the Church of England to Catholicism. In the story of Elizabeth Prout and the founding of the Sisters of the Cross and Passion we enter another story in the English Catholic Church historical context, and eventually into its Irish chapter. The threads of this story and the founding values of this woman and her companions will weave with those of Frances Taylor and Genevieve Dupuis, and with the other founding stories in the reconfiguration of the Le Chéile Trust.

Elizabeth Prout was born in Coleham, Shrewsbury on 2 September 1820. The daughter of a lapsed Roman Catholic father and a devout Anglican mother, Elizabeth was baptised in the Church of England. The brewery in Stone where Elizabeth's father, Edward Prout, worked closed down in 1831, and it is believed that the family had to move to a number of different locations as he sought alternative employment. Elizabeth was born into an England of both active anti-Roman Catholicism and growing Roman Catholic revival. Catholic Relief Acts were being passed and French immigrant priests and religious were arriving in England. The Irish post-famine 'invasion' added other threads to the founding context with the arrival of numbers of impoverished families and committed devotional Catholics.

Dominic Barberi is the second central figure in the founding story of the Cross and Passion Sisters. Born and reared in Italy, he became a priest and led the Passionist Mission to England. He established the first English Passionist community at Aston Hall, two miles from Stone, in 1842. He accepted charge of Aston Parish and rented a room in Stone's Crown Inn where he celebrated Mass on Sundays. People, some curious, some looking for entertainment, some interested, went to hear Barberi. It was a difficult time for the mission and there are accounts of how Barberi and his companions were often insulted and stoned as they made their way to celebrate Mass. Elizabeth's life was changed by listening to and meeting with Barberi and she was received into the Catholic Church in 1846. Interestingly, Barberi had received John Henry Newman into the Roman Catholic Church in the previous year, 1845.

Elizabeth's parents were unhappy with her decision to become a Catholic and she was disowned by them for some time. She spent a short time in a convent but when diagnosed with a tubercular condition she returned to her home where her parents welcomed her back. Once again she made the choice of the Catholic faith, and on the advice of another Passionist priest, Fr Gaudentius, went to Manchester where she secured a teaching post in the parish of St Chad. Alone and in a city teeming with famine-afflicted Irish immigrants she, with some other young women and under Fr Gaudentius' direction, began to work in Stocks Street, Manchester.

In 1852 this new group of English women religious was formally launched. Elizabeth with six companions received a formal religious dress in St Chad's Church. We are told that because they were so poor they dyed their own clothes black. Indeed, a new religious community was born in poverty and for the poor.

Dire poverty, a context of sectarian troubles and the regular desecration of Catholic churches presented many challenges for the new religious community. It was a difficult mission and some of Elizabeth's companions gradually lost heart and left the group. Of the six Sisters who were professed as religious with Elizabeth only one persevered, Mother Mary Paul Taylor, a convert from Methodism.

The new community focused on educating the poor. Elizabeth believed, as other founders did, that without education the poor could not achieve the potential for which they were created. She wanted them to have a political voice. When Sr Máire Ní Shuilleabháin, a Cross and Passion congregational member, was asked about the core purpose in Elizabeth Prout's mission, she replied: 'Education, because the foundress recognised that in order for people to live independent lives they had to have education. In her time in England there was no education for Catholics.'

Fr Ignatius Spencer, an English gentry convert and great-grand-uncle of the late Diana, Princess of Wales, was appointed guardian of the struggling new community. Spencer had a similar experience to Elizabeth as he too had been disowned by his family when he became a Roman Catholic. This new Passionist leader provided gentle and supportive guardianship for the Sisters. Just ten years after Elizabeth's death in 1864, the Passionist Fathers allowed the name of the new community of women to be changed to 'Sisters of the Cross and Passion', and gave permission for the Sisters to wear the Passionist Sign. In the context of the transfer of Passionist values into the Sisters' congregation, Fr Barberi and the English missionaries contributed to the dream of their founder, St Paul of the Cross, to renew the English Catholic Church. The Congregation of the Cross and Passion Sisters received Rome's approbation of the Rule in 1887.

On the occasion of the 1998 Pilgrimage to Elizabeth's shrine in Shrewsbury, Fr Nicholas Postlethwaite, Passionist Provincial, suggested that Elizabeth Prout's womanly insights, her analysis of the English society of her time, and her daily living with the poor had enabled her to develop and deepen the original Passionist vision, theology and spirit.

A headline in *The Daily Telegraph* on 27 June 2008 declared, 'Nun Elizabeth Prout could become saint,' with the subheading, 'A nun who helped educate women in the slums of Manchester is being put forward to become a saint.' The article includes a statement by Fr Barry McAllister, a Liverpool priest who had been involved in preparing the Cause of Sr Elizabeth Prout, and who describes her as 'a great forerunner of women's rights and of women having a role in society'.

The Cross and Passion Sisters came to Ireland in 1878, to Kilcullen, Co. Kildare. The congregation's website provides an interesting piece of history:

> In 1868 Cardinal Cullen appointed Fr Langan to Kilcullen to assist the aging Fr Murtagh, whom he succeeded as parish priest in 1872. He ministered in Kilcullen for thirty-five years. In 1874 the Sisters of the Holy Faith established a community in Liffeybank near Kilcullen. However, their tenancy was precarious. The landlord, it would appear, felt that Kilcullen at that time needed a doctor more than teachers and accordingly the Sisters of the Holy Faith departed in 1877 to make way for the new occupant – a Doctor Barker. Canon Langan, however, was determined. He invited the Sisters of the Cross & Passion and succeeded in obtaining for them a suitable house – donated by one Thomas Quinn. This man also later gave enough land for a new convent and a loan of money for building. By September 1878 the house was ready ... the Sisters were conducted in procession by the enthusiastic Parish Priest [...] Work started immediately in the National School [...] making visitations to the poor. The Sisters also opened a private boarding school for girls in their temporary convent, the original number of pupils being three (crossandpassion.com).

The Holy Faith Sisters, too, had lived and worked in Kilcullen. They departed in 1873 when their Protestant landlord refused to renew the lease, but five years later the Cross and Passion Sisters arrived. Two religious congregations, the Holy Faith Sisters and the Cross and Passion Sisters, are now weaving together in the foundation of the Le Chéile Trust, ensuring the future of their Catholic secondary schools in Ireland.

Gerry Wrigley, principal of Maryfield College, an Irish Cross and Passion school in Glandore Road, Dublin, spoke warmly of Elizabeth Prout, of the founding story of the congregation and of the core values in that story:

> I think the first value would be the fact that Elizabeth Prout's vocational calling was in the area of female education and an acknowledgement of what women could contribute and were entitled to be allowed to contribute to society. And I think that is

always something that we have had in the school. The idea of women's worth in society and the role we can play with twelve-year-olds coming into the school and then leaving as eighteen-year-old women playing a full part in society.

He went on to speak of the founder's love for and service to the poor. The students in his school are involved with the Hope Foundation: 'they work with the Street Children in Calcutta, and also with the Cross and Passion Sisters' community in Peru'. It would seem that Elizabeth Prout's values of commitment to faith, to education for girls and to love for the poor are living in her schools in the twenty-first century.

The challenge is to allow God to work through us. Our ministries are an expression of our Mission.

IN IRELAND CROSS AND PASSION / LE CHÉILE SCHOOLS ARE:

- Cross and Passion College, Kilcullen, Co. Kildare.
- Maryfield College, Glandore Road, Dublin.

THE POOR SERVANTS OF THE MOTHER OF GOD

Not though the soldier knew
Someone had blundered ...
Theirs but to do and die.
Into the valley of Death
Rode the six hundred.

Tennyson's celebration of the infamous *Charge of the Light Brigade* in the Crimean War in 1854 is the sad but central context for the founding story of the Poor Servants of the Mother of God. Frances Taylor, a young Anglican volunteer nurse, had travelled to the Crimea to assist Florence Nightingale in the medical care of the English army. Twenty per cent of the tragic English Light Brigade were Irish men. They, with their English companions, were led into certain death because of a scandalously ill-advised direction given by their military leaders. The wounded were nursed by the Nightingale team and also by the Irish Mercy Sisters who had journeyed to the Crimea to care for the soldiers. Frances Taylor, who originally joined Nightingale, was gradually drawn to work with the Irish Mercy Sisters. She was attracted to their faith and found them self-sacrificing, uncomplaining, tireless and yet alive with a quiet joy which lifted the atmosphere in every ward they nursed in. She was also significantly influenced by the faith of the fatally-injured young Irish men for whom she wrote letters of final farewell to their families in Ireland. She would later refer to the fact that it was their faith that challenged her to convert to Catholicism.

Frances Taylor was born in Stoke Rochford, Lincolnshire, in 1832. She was the youngest of ten children of Henry Taylor, an Anglican Rector of a rural Lincolnshire parish, and his wife Louisa Maria Jones. Frances' paternal grandfather, Richard Taylor, had been rector of parishes in Wiltshire and Hampshire. On her mother's side, her family were merchants and shopkeepers in the City of London. Her father, a graduate of Lincoln College, Oxford, had been a curate at St Mary Abbots, Kensington. Naturally her father's faith and parish life were of first importance to her. Sundays were set aside for Scripture reading and church attendance, and her mother's diaries tell of Frances's readiness to accompany her when she visited the sick or the elderly poor. Financially the family were comfortable, but not well-off. We can deduce this when we read in her mother's diary that when she planned to send for the doctor to see her sick husband on one occasion, he worried about paying the doctor's fee. Louisa Taylor wrote in her diary on 1 March 1842: 'Oh, may it please God to relieve his mind upon pecuniary matters, for our pocket is very low.'

After her father's death, the Taylor family moved to London. In the 1840s, London was a city with extremes of wealth and poverty. Frances began her charitable work in the city's workhouses. She developed a desire to serve the poor and vulnerable. In 1848 her sisters Emma and Charlotte had joined an Anglican Sisterhood, the Sisters of Mercy of the Holy Trinity. Frances followed suit around 1852, as a 'visitor', and she appears to have stayed for two years. She may have been involved in nurse training at Bristol, and she developed her nursing vocation serving in Plymouth during the cholera epidemic of 1853.

Frances was just twenty-two years of age and still searching for meaning in life when the Crimean War began in 1854. Russia had decided to carve up Turkey and in this was opposed by England and France. News of the war and injured soldiers reached London so Frances volunteered for nursing and journeyed to a military hospital in the war zone. She was accepted for the second party of volunteer nurses which went out in December 1854, being joined later by her sister Charlotte in April 1855. She nursed for a short time with Florence Nightingale at Scutari Hospital but was critical of the organisation, particularly of supplies at the hospital. She shortly moved to another military hospital at Koulali. It was at this hospital that she met with the Irish Sisters of Mercy and the young Irish soldiers. Due to this extraordinary event she would be converted to Catholicism and, eventually, received into the Church. Frances was later to say that her experience of nursing these young men so far from home and the way they expressed their faith as she wrote their letters was significant in her conversion to Catholicism. In her conversion process she sought the advice of Fr Sydney Woollett SJ, who was assisting the hospital Catholic chaplain. She was received into the Catholic Church by Fr Woollett on 14 April 1855.

This brave young nurse was also a literary scholar and author. She pursued her own writing when time permitted. On returning to London she published her first book, *Eastern Hospitals and English Nurses*. This was an account of her wartime experiences and was one of the earliest published eye-witness accounts of the military hospitals. The book in its final edition in 1857 included an impassioned appeal for reform of the public nursing system, and in general of the treatment of the poor by contemporary society. As a Catholic in post-Penal England she recognised the dearth of Catholic publications and she began to write a monthly magazine featuring the work of other Catholic writers.

Cardinal Manning, the newly-appointed leader of the Catholic Church in England, became Frances' spiritual director. He guided her into working with London's unemployed girls, maidservants, factory workers and seamstresses. Frances soon identified the provision of schools as the most immediate need for the young London poor women. Sr Kathleen Coleman describes this significant period in Frances' life:

> After the war, she returned to London and because it was a time of great poverty, it was the time of Dickens, she noticed the number of children on the street with nowhere to go. They had no shoes, they were badly clad, and she took pity on them and she set up little

'hedge-schools', you could call them, little schools for them, in order to at least teach them the catechism, and to give them some kind of a meal.

Frances believed that there was a clear link between criminal activities, anti-social behaviour and the lack of educational opportunity. She even encouraged the children to attend school by providing them with bread and treacle.

In 1866 Frances was thinking of founding a religious group of women to work with her among the poor. She travelled to Ireland to visit newly-founded Irish congregations. To pay for her trip, and to help the English reading public understand the Irish character and the injustices suffered by the Irish people in their own land, Frances continued writing monthly articles. The popular articles were collected into one volume and in 1867 were published as *Irish Homes and Irish Hearts*. The author dedicated her work 'to those who – under strange skies taught me the worth of Irish character, the warmth of Irish hearts and depth of Irish faith'.

Frances continued to search for a clear focus in her life. She discussed religious vocation with advisors and visited many convents. A visit to Polish religious congregations in 1869 was a seminal experience for her because she realised she should found her own congregation to meet the needs of the poor in England. After thirteen years of searching the Poor Servants of the Mother of God Congregation was formally established near Tower Hill London, on 24 September 1869.

Her affection for the Irish contributed to Frances' desire to have a convent in Ireland. Initial efforts were not successful but eventually she received an invitation from Fr Seymour, parish priest of Carrigtwohill, Co. Cork, who expressed the desire to have 'one of your little convents established in this small town or village'. He offered the sisters a site for the convent and promised them 'the grass for a cow'. In 1875 Frances Taylor's sisters arrived. The Poor Servants of the Mother of God then began their educational mission in Ireland, bringing their founding values of courage, generosity, love for the poor and an educational mission. These are the gifts in their charism which are now entrusted to Le Chéile.

Frances Taylor met the needs of her time in the London of the nineteenth century. Mary O'Neill, principal of one of Frances' schools in Ireland, Manor House, Raheny, aptly summarises that inspiration: 'If you adopt the Frances Taylor maxim, you will develop and change and meet the needs, because the needs are changing all the time.'

An interesting thread in this foundation story is that, as Cornelia Connelly was beginning her new congregation, Frances Taylor was going to the Crimea. She would return to Dickensian London to found the Poor Servants of the Mother of God, Elizabeth Prout was in Manchester about to found the Cross and Passion Sisters, and Fr Tandy, in Birmingham, was inviting Genevieve Dupuis to found the Sisters of Charity of St Paul the Apostle. All four women were concerned about the needs of the time, poverty, education and faith. One is struck by a love and commitment to the mission of Jesus Christ and a clear commitment to education in the founding, and in the development of the four English Le Chéile congregations.

The Poor Servants of the Mother of God believe that Mother Magdalen Taylor's great contribution to education was the energy she exerted in establishing orphanages where Catholic orphans who had been consigned to Protestant workhouses would be, with the help of Cardinal Manning, saved for the Catholic Church by being placed in the orphanages which she established, and thus brought up as Catholics.

Following in the footsteps of Mother Magdalen, we are attracted to the God who became one of us. Each day we strive anew to reach out with the compassion and love of Jesus.

IN IRELAND POOR SERVANTS OF THE MOTHER OF GOD /
LE CHÉILE SCHOOLS ARE:

- St Aloysius College, Carrigtwohill, Co. Cork.
- Manor House School, Raheny, Dublin.

Historical Context for the French Le Chéile Congregations

Five of the original Le Chéile congregations, the De La Salle Brothers, the Religious of Christian Education, the Religious of Jesus and Mary, the Faithful Companions of Jesus and the St Louis Sisters, were founded in France. Another of the congregations which has joined the Trust since 2009, the Sisters of St Joseph of Cluny, is also of French origin. Le Chéile therefore, has a rich inheritance from the country that has been called 'the eldest daughter of the Church'. Prior to the French Revolution in 1789 the Catholic Church was the official State religion, and the King of France was known as 'His Most Christian Majesty'.

Historians agree that the seventeenth century was what they call 'a great century' for France and the Church. There are even references to a period of 'religious splendour'. New religious congregations such as the Brothers founded by St John Baptist de La Salle began at this time. The French school of spirituality, which reached a peak in this century, was concerned with raising the standard of the diocesan clergy in line with the decrees of the Council of Trent (1545–63). But there were also challenges, a religious restlessness and signs of spiritual unrest. Galileo's scientific findings and courageous defense of his new knowledge influenced religion and philosophy, as well as science and mathematics. With the earth out of its central privileged position, other long-held beliefs came under scrutiny and suspicion too.

Official Catholicism, distrust of Rome, and state interventionism were the main components of French eighteenth-century Catholic Church history. Louis XIV died in 1715, a year that marked a wave of irreligion beginning to sweep through the country. In the following decades the philosophers imposed themselves on French cultural life. Rationalism, negative criticism of all religion, especially Catholicism, and a general attitude of intellectual rebellion shaped the 'enlightenment' of eighteenth-century France. The majority of ordinary people kept their faith and its practice but the small minority of intellectual philosophers were significantly influential in the changing culture.

François-Marie Arouet, known by his nom de plume Voltaire, was a French writer, historian and philosopher famous for his wit, his attacks on the established Catholic Church, and his advocacy of freedom of religion, of expression and the separation of the French Church and State. He produced works in almost every literary form including plays, poems, novels, essays, and historical and scientific works. He wrote more than 20,000 letters and published more than 2,000 books and pamphlets. His ambition was to eliminate the Christian religion, but ironically he, himself, acted the role of a 'high priest'. Those elements of philosophy, new theories and regular publication of polemical writing provided the seeds for an era of revolution at the end of the eighteenth century. This era would change the course of French and European history.

Voltaire did not have the philosophical field to himself. His influence was somewhat balanced by the foundational work of the German philosopher Immanuel Kant, who argued for the unique freedom and power of one's own reason. Blaise Pascal, too, argued that God's approach to man was through revelation, religious experience and the Judeo–Christian tradition as well as through reason. These theoretical threads weave in and through the historical context for the foundation of the French Le Chéile congregations.

France occupied the centre of the world stage at the end of the eighteenth and the beginning of the nineteenth centuries, a position which was to be of significant importance for the destinies of Catholicism and the Church. It might be argued that the final grand staging of the relationship between Church and State was a solemn procession in 1789 presided over by King Louis XVI with representatives from the three estates (clergy, nobility and commoners) holding candles and devoutly following the Blessed Sacrament. This was to be followed by a radical, swift, political and religious rebellion. Experiencing the poverty and economic crisis exacerbated by ongoing wars the common people of France had become increasingly frustrated by the ineptitude of the king and the perceived decadence of the aristocracy. This resentment, coupled with the theories of Voltaire and his followers fueled the radical sentiments. The next ten years were dominated by struggles between left and right assemblies and groups, and by many atrocities within an internal revolution.

The Catholic Church was directly affected when on 13 February 1790 a decision was taken to suppress monastic vows, and on 12 July the Assembly approved the Civil Constitution of the Clergy. A new French Church was created, independent of papal authority, and priests were required to swear fidelity to the new political constitution. Pope Pius VI excommunicated priests who took the oath and a schism ensued. In 1792 the non-juring priests were deported, and in September of that year many priests were executed. In January 1793 Louis XVI was executed and in the same year Christian holidays, including Sunday, were suppressed. Anti-Catholic actions included churches being turned into Temples of Reason and a statue of the Goddess of Reason set up in Notre Dame Cathedral in Paris. When the French occupied Rome and Pope Pius VI died in exile (1799), some revolutionaries boasted that the last pope had died.

In November 1799 Napoleon Bonaparte became First Consul of France, and four months later Pope Pius VII was elected pope. A concordat was agreed between the Pope and Napoleon on 15 July 1801, and a new episcopacy was created permitting a Catholic faith life to be redeveloped. Seminaries, financially supported by the State, were founded but Napoleon continued to be very restrictive with regard to religious congregations. This was the State and Church into which five of the French Le Chéile congregations were born. The consequences of the Revolution itself were the contextual motivations for those who gathered others to defend the faith, develop it and provide schools for this mission.

The De La Salle Brothers

A chance encounter between a young priest and a zealous layman in Reims, France, in 1679 led to the founding of an educational project which is now worldwide. The layman, Adrian Nyel, who at that time was interested in setting up a school in Reims for poor boys, gladly welcomed the assistance of this educated influential priest, John Baptist de La Salle. In this simple visit a unique Le Chéile congregation began. This was the seminal moment for the beginning of the first non-clerical congregation of men dedicated to faith and education, the congregation we know in Ireland as the De La Salle Brothers. The man who offered educational assistance that day in Reims was to become a renowned educational reformer and be recognised as the father of modern pedagogy.

John Baptist de La Salle was born into a prosperous merchant family in Reims on 30 April 1651. He was educated by the Jesuits and completed a master's degree at the age of eighteen. In the following year he joined a seminary in Paris, and began studying theology in the Sorbonne. He completed a doctorate in theology in 1680, having been ordained a priest two years earlier. On the death of his parents he returned to Reims to care for his younger brothers and sisters. He balanced both the responsibilities of family with his pastoral efforts to renew the Church according to the decrees of the Council of Trent. This ecumenical council was responding to the development of Protestantism and its main objective was to define Catholic doctrine and reform numerous abuses within the Catholic Church.

Prior to a request to assist Adrian Nyel, he had no intention of focusing on education as a key ministry, and, initially, did not consciously set out to become directly involved. However, the poor children being educated in Reims and other areas won both his heart and his attention and the central mission of his life began. Other men joined him. He directed and supported them and eventually realised that together they needed a home. Thus emerged the De La Salle religious community.

John Baptist De La Salle's life spanned the years of France's 'great century' but it was also a time of poverty and unrest as a consequence of years of warfare. At the same time the Church was dealing with the challenges of the Jansenists who were emphasising original sin, human depravity and predestination. This was the France within which de La Salle's life work of teaching, providing schools and training teachers to work in these schools was beginning. The De La Salle Brothers were the first non-clerical Roman Catholic religious teaching congregation. His enterprise met opposition from the ecclesiastical authorities who resisted the creation of this new form of religious life. The educational establishment resented his innovative methods and his insistence on receiving children of all social classes. Nevertheless de La Salle and his Brothers succeeded in creating a network of quality schools throughout France. The schools featured instruction in the vernacular, grouping of students according to ability and achievement, integration of religious instruction with secular subjects, well-prepared teachers with a sense of vocation and mission, and the involvement of parents. He was a pioneer in his programmes for training lay-teachers. For this purpose he founded a training college in Reims in 1685.

John Baptist de La Salle is recognised as a pedagogical innovator whose theories would later influence, among others, both Pestalozzi and Froebel. He founded one of the first institutions in France for the care of delinquents as well as technical schools and secondary schools for modern languages, arts, sciences, and Sunday courses for young working men. By insisting on the vernacular rather than Latin as the basis for instruction he opened up national literature and history for the young students. He would be considered historically one of the great practical pioneers of education for ordinary people, first in France and later in the rest of the world. His imaginative ideas, the schools he founded and the reforms he made in teaching methods completely changed the educational system.

Br Stephen Deignan, a former congregational leader, proudly summarises his founder's contribution:

> As he became aware by God's grace of the human and spiritual distress of the children of artisans and the poor, John Baptist de La Salle devoted himself to forming school masters totally devoted to teaching and Christian education. He brought these teachers together in a community and subsequently founded with them the Brothers of the Christian Schools.

This was the name given to the formal group in France at the time of their founding.

The De La Salle Brothers came to Ireland in 1880, to an Ireland of land agitation, evictions and agrarian crime. The Le Chéile tapestry shows knotted threads in the complicated first step in this mission. Bishop Gillooly of Elphin had identified the need to establish a home for orphaned and neglected children. He had built Summerhill College in Athlone. Br Joachim O'Callaghan was vocation-questing in Ireland in 1880 and Bishop Gillooly took the opportunity to invite the Brothers to take over the College in Summerhill. Difficulties developed with both the government inspector, Sir John Lentaigne, and with the bishop. That project failed but it did give the Brothers a sense of the needs of the Irish poor. Br Stephen develops this point:

> Our initial schools were all poorer schools in a sense that they were the schools for towns and villages throughout the country, which were poor, I am thinking of places like Ballaghaderreen and Ballyshannon and Waterford at that particular time … it is important to realise as well that our second opening in Ireland was a training college and that would have come as a result of knowledge of the training colleges in France at that time because de La Salle himself had opened quite a number of training colleges when he saw how inadequate training for the teachers was at that time, and his main foundational element was teams of well-trained teachers.

Within three months of leaving Summerhill in 1882, the Brothers had founded their novitiate at Castletown, Co. Laois. The Brothers founded a training college for lay teachers in Waterford in 1891 which continued in existence until 1948. Thus began a weaving of the founding threads of the De La Salle schools in Ireland. Within this story the founding values of John Baptist de La Salle's congregation and schools are identified. By default he founded the first non-clerical religious congregation to meet the needs he had identified. Joe Twomey, former principal of Beneavin De La Salle College, Dublin, confidently claims:

> When Lasallians get together we talk about the values being taught, that they are there in the school … the kids pick the values up without knowing it. So we want them to be good Christian people at the end of their five years in Beneavin school, and we want them also to have a very strong knowledge that they are fortunate, because they have been to a Lasallian school.

In 1950 Pope Pius XII proclaimed John Baptist de La Salle 'Special Patron of all Christian Educators'.

In Ireland De La Salle / Le Chéile schools are:

- Árdscoil La Salle, Raheny, Dublin.
- Beneavin De La Salle College, Dublin.
- De La Salle College, Churchtown, Dublin.
- De La Salle College, Waterford.
- De La Salle Secondary School, Dundalk, Co Louth.
- St Benildus College, Kilmacud, Co. Dublin.
- St John's College De La Salle, Ballyfermot, Dublin.
- St Gerald's College, Castlebar, Co. Mayo.

THE ST JOSEPH OF CLUNY SISTERS

A pretty, precocious and spoilt child is the central character early in the story of the St Joseph of Cluny Sisters. Anne-Marie, or Nanette as she was affectionately called, developed into a young woman who would defy her father, found a religious congregation, liberate slaves, and be excommunicated by a local bishop.

Anne-Marie was born on 10 November 1779. Balthazar Javouhey, her father, was the owner of a rich property at Chamblanc in east-central France. Her mother, Claudine Parisot, was a deeply religious woman who gave a religious significance to everything in her life. Balthazar and Claudine having suffered the death and loss of four previous children welcomed the birth of their cherished Anne-Marie. She would eventually have three younger sisters and a brother, and her life would be intimately involved with her siblings. She, however, was undoubtedly the leader. She was a joy to her parents, and her childhood was spent within a happy family. Some who knew the family thought that the young Nanette was too worldly for the daughter of so pious a couple as Balthazar and Claudine, and there was also a sense that she was being spoilt.

Anne-Marie was ten years old when the French Revolution began in 1789. This was a time when churches and schools were closed, and priests, religious and believers were persecuted. It was under these circumstances that the young girl became more aware of the spiritual needs of the people around her. Like many families in France at the time, the Javouheys did not take an active political side in the events convulsing their country. The Revolution created widespread poverty, and Balthazar struggled to keep his farms and business operating. Like other Catholic families, Balthazar and Claudine were supportive of the priests and religious who opposed the ruling of the Civil Constitution of the Clergy which demanded an oath of allegiance to the State. Anne-Marie assisted her parents in the protection of their priests. When a priest was not available for Mass, the Jahouvey family and their Catholic neighbours gathered at various homes to recite the Rosary or to read the prayers of the Mass. Anne-Marie, a teenager, was becoming more responsible. She recognised that because Catholic schools were unlawful the younger children in the area were without any formal religious teaching. This inspired her to begin her life's work, teaching catechism. Her personality began to change, too, as she became less interested in worldly attractions. This was a period when her loving father was frustrated by her behaviours. He tried in vain to arrange a good and suitable marriage for her. She withdrew from what might be considered a normal life for a young woman. She began reading spiritual books at meal times. Her sisters followed her example, and even those who worked in Balthazar's farms and business were influenced by her spiritual exercises. One might feel some sympathy for the boss – Anne-Marie's father.

The catechism classes for children continued, and adults were soon coming to her for spiritual guidance. Because her father was not pleased with the radical changes which were taking place both in family and among his employees, Anne-Marie moved into the home of her brother Etienne. She would later return to her father's home and even persuade him to give her permission to open a school there. In his mind a school was better than having his daughter enter a convent.

She was now coping with large numbers of orphans, young victims of the Revolution. With the exception of a few women who came in occasionally to help, Nanette did all the teaching, the cooking, the housework, the laundry and the care of the children. It was her father, once again, who came to her assistance. He suggested that Nanette and the children move to Chablanc where he could be of more direct help. Balthazar built a school, paid the bills and half the family home became a convent. During the visit of Pope Pius VII to France, Anne-Marie was able to speak briefly to him about her work. With his approval and his encouragement, she began thinking of founding her own congregation. Two years later, on 12 May 1807, Bishop Imberties of Autun officially bestowed religious habits upon Anne-Marie and eight other women, including three of her sisters. This act officially founded the Society of St Joseph. 'Cluny' was only added in 1812 when a large house   in Cluny, France, was bought by the ever-patient and generous Balthazar. This became the principal house of the new congregation. Anne-Marie was only twenty-eight years old when the congregation was formally launched. As fast as she could provide Sisters, new convents and schools were opened.

The Sisters cared for orphans, educated children and worked for the human development of all. As the new congregation and its related schools grew in reputation, the Governor of the island of Bourbon (present-day Réunion), who had come to France looking for teachers, asked Anne-Marie to send Sisters to educate the indigenous children of Bourbon. She recognised this request as an opportunity to fulfil her missionary vocation. Without hesitation she accepted, and sent a third of her Sisters to the remote island in the Indian Ocean in January 1817. This was the beginning of rapid missionary expansion of the St Joseph of Cluny Congregation. Two years later the Sisters arrived in Saint-Louis, Senegal, and their mission continued to spread. In 1836 the Sisters were welcomed to the West Indies, and some time later they established houses in Tahiti.

One of Anne-Marie's most significant missionary initiatives was the formation of the African clergy. She passionately believed in the need for African men to be educated and trained as priests for their own people. Anne-Marie also worked tirelessly for the liberation of slaves in the new countries to which she and her Sisters travelled and provided schools and services. In her own lifetime, her missionary activities were extended to the five continents. She was acclaimed as the 'Liberator of Slaves', and 'Mother of Black Races'.

Despite her total dedication to the mission of Jesus Christ Anne-Marie Janouhey was submitted to an ultimate Church punishment when, in the 1840s, she was excommunicated. During this time she was not permitted to receive the Sacraments, and this she was later to say was the greatest deprivation for her. The humiliation was imposed on her because she would not agree to a local bishop's demand to sign a document which would have changed the governance of her congregation. The excommunication was lifted after two years and she was visited and honoured by priests, bishops and royalty. Anne-Marie Javouhey died in 1851.

In 1850 Anne-Marie was invited to Ireland 'to teach the poor and the well-to-do'. She agreed believing that 'we could do some good there'. Ten years later the Sisters of St Joseph of Cluny came to Ireland at the request of Fr Leman, a Holy Ghost father and founder of Blackrock College, and with the approval and support of Archbishop Paul Cullen. Mount Sackville Girls' boarding school was opened in 1864.

Cluny schools follow in the footsteps of Christ and of Anne-Marie Javouhey.

They [the Sisters] bring about liberation from ignorance, ill health and sinful social structures through various apostolates in different parts of the world.

In Ireland St Joseph of Cluny / Le Chéile schools are:

- St Joseph of Cluny Secondary School, Killiney, Co. Dublin.
- Mount Sackville Secondary School, Chapelizod, Co. Dublin.

THE SISTERS OF ST LOUIS

It was the feast of the Sacred Heart, June 1797, and in the old feudal manor of Turquenstein on a peak of the French Vosges mountains, a man and two women sat around a small table. Their names, Abbé Louis Colmar, Louise Humann and Thérèse Breck; they were deeply devout people living in post-Revolution France. Conscious of a persecuted Church and a fragmented war-torn people they reflected on Scripture and prayed. They signed a document of unity to live and effect the prayer 'sint unum – may all be one', taken from Our Lord's prayer at the last supper (John 17:22). Their promise to God and to each other was that the education of youth would achieve what they desired, and within this simple, unique and signed promise was the seed of founding for the St Louis Sisters.

Sr Mary O'Connor, a former congregational leader describes the Turquenstein foundational meeting:

> They dedicated themselves to the Sacred Heart of Jesus and to working for education. They had just experienced the French Revolution and all the persecution of Catholics during that time. Louis Colmar was living the life of a fugitive priest. They saw the necessity for education, it was key and it was only through having an educated Catholic laity that they were going to be able to preserve the faith in France.

The advent of Napoleon Bonaparte saw some of the worst features of the persecution of religious practice removed. Among the bishops approved by Napoleon was Abbé Colmar who was appointed to the See of Mayence in 1801. In 1801 he invited Humann and Breck to take responsibility for educational ministry in his diocese. They established a large boarding school, one which was to draw its pupils from the foremost French and German families of the town and surrounding district. Louise Humann was described as a 'born teacher', her first students had been her younger brothers and sisters. Her educational abilities and skills were complemented by her deep love for the children and she created within her school a family spirit for the students. This spirit became the hallmark of educational houses by her followers. Religious education held the first place in the programmes of the schools which were to follow. Louise was educating young girls for life, and their faith was integral to that training.

In 1821, Louis Bautain entered the St Louis founding story. He was a professor of philosophy. As a young man studying in post-Revolution Paris he had been influenced by the free-thinking philosophy of the time and had abandoned his childhood faith. He met Louise Humann and under her guidance and influence he began to take an interest in religious questions. He returned to the Catholic faith and was ordained a priest in 1828. Louise introduced him to the philosophical legacy of Abbé Colmar who had inspired her. After the death of Bishop Colmar, Louise returned to Strasburg and became the centre of a circle of bourgeois academics, among them Louis Bautain. These brilliant young men were inspired by the Pact of Turquenstein and by Louise's gentle care, devotion and strong faith.

Bautain set himself the task of healing the deep and supposedly irreconcilable divisions that existed between faith and reason and between theology and popular secular learning. He came to the conclusion that education, what he called 'the beautiful enterprise', was the great need of the day. After Louise's death, Bautain and the group, many of whom were now ordained priests, moved to Juilly, hear Paris, where Bautain, with the help of the Baronne de Vaux (Mère Thérèse de la Croix), founded the Sisters of St Louis in 1842. Education was the primary mission of the Sisters of St Louis and Louis Bautain guided the Sisters at every step. *Ut sint unum* was the motto of the new congregation and of all St Louis schools.

In 1859 the St Louis Sisters arrived in Monaghan, Ireland, at the invitation of Dr McNally, Bishop of Clogher, who had pleaded with Louis Bautain to make the foundation. One of the Sisters was English, two were Irish, all were former students of the St Louis boarding school in Juilly. Sr Mary O'Connor explains that: 'At that time there was a remarkable amount of coming and going between Ireland and France. There was the Irish College in Paris. A number of girls, from Ireland, entered St Louis in France before 1859.'

In Monaghan the Sisters established a reformatory for girls in need. The Sisters were also invited to establish schools for Catholics who could afford to pay for education. Previously the children of these families were attending a local Protestant school in Monaghan. The Sisters extended their mission to the poor and destitute.

An unexpected difficulty arose for the early Sisters in Monaghan. The local Irish bishop and Louis Bautain disagreed on the actual status of the new foundation. The vexed question related to control of the new foundation in Ireland. Mère Thérèse's instructions were explicit, the Sisters were to remain linked to their original foundation or return to Juilly. Louis Bautain, conscious of the importance of the mission in Monaghan, and after visiting the foundation there twice asked the Sisters to sacrifice their direct link to Juilly but to remain attached *in spirit*. The Monaghan Sisters had to cut their founding 'umbilical cord'. This was a difficult challenge/choice. Nonetheless, the Sisters remained steadfast to their mission in Ireland.

But the story comes full circle. In the mid-twentieth century Monaghan and Juilly were reunited under the one governance. While French culture and heritage were always strong in St Louis schools, they were also to the fore in promoting Gaelic culture, language and heritage.

The mission of the Sisters of St Louis is motivated primarily by the Mission of Christ and our Charism 'Sint Unum – May all be One' calls us to grow towards oneness in Christ and to foster right relationships with God and the whole of creation.

In Ireland Sisters of St Louis / Le Chéile schools are:

- St Louis Secondary School, Monaghan
- St Louis Secondary School, Carrickmacross, Co. Monaghan
- St Louis Secondary School, Dundalk, Co. Louth
- St Louis High School, Rathmines, Dublin

The St Louis Sisters also act as partner trustee in:

- Blakestown Community School, Co. Dublin (with Servite Fathers, and Dublin VEC).
- Ramsgrange Community School, Co. Wexford (with Co. Wexford VEC).
- St Louis Community School, Kiltimagh, Co. Mayo (with Mayo VEC).

The Faithful Companions of Jesus

Marie-Madeleine d'Houët's journey from Society wife and widow to religious founder is a complex one. She was born into the aristocratic, royalist de Bengy family in Chateauroux, France in 1781 and was caught up in the atrocities of the French Revolution when her father was imprisoned and she, her mother, brother and sister went into hiding.

In 1804 Marie-Madeleine d'Houët married Joseph de Bonnault d'Houët whose family background was very like her own. Theirs was the experience of a vast social, economic and religious change taking place in their country as it moved from an 'ancien regime' culture to a post-revolutionary society. Wishing to respond to the needs of the poor, Marie Madeleine and Joseph volunteered to assist in a local hospital. It was there that Joseph contracted typhoid fever and died. They had been married for just eleven months. Three months later their son Eugène was born.

Initially she suffered intense post-natal depression but gradually returned to her former way of life describing herself at this time as the most doting of mothers. Marie Madeleine, now a mother, daughter and daughter-in-law, was also a business woman responsible for overseeing the household needs and managing the vineyards she inherited. When the time came for Eugène to go to school she chose to send him to the newly-restored St Acheul in Amiens under the direction of the Jesuit Fathers. Such was her devotion to her son that she went with him and took rooms in the town to be near him. Inevitably she came under the influence of the

Jesuits and when Fr Varin, a former Royalist officer, was proclaimed as being on the 'wanted' list during the 'Hundred Days' (the period between Emperor Napoleon I of France's return from exile on Elba to Paris and the second restoration of King Louis XVIII in 1815) she did not hesitate to offer him shelter on her country estate. He spent three months at Parassy, Berry. In that secluded place their conversation turned often on the Society of Jesus, its spirituality and mission. Madame d'Houët tried to balance her maternal and business responsibilities with her search for God's will in her life. She was much attracted to religious life and even thought of entering Carmel.

Eventually, on the feast of the Sacred Heart of Jesus, 13 June 1817, God showed her the way forward. In response to the words 'I THIRST' which she heard from the crucifix over the altar, she knelt and offered herself with all her heart for whatever God might ask of her. She said later in life that what she had experienced was the thirst of Jesus, a thirst for the salvation of souls. A few days later another experience showed her that she was to become a companion of Jesus and found a society of women religious for the education of children and the work of retreats and missions. On the feast of the Visitation, on the way to Mass, she knew definitively that she was given four companions whom she was to cherish and from whom she was never to part. These companions were 'Humility, Poverty, Obedience and Gentleness.'

During the summer of 1818, Madame d'Houët was invited to the home of Fr Varin's sister, only to find that Madame Barat, founder of the Religious of the Sacred Heart was also invited. Fr Varin had constantly put pressure on Marie Madeleine to join that Society and it was his intention to exert pressure once again. She however received another light:

> I cannot be a Jesuit ... But no, I will not be outdone. Wait a while; my name is Magdalen. I will follow my patron saint, who so loved Jesus as to accompany him in his journeys and his labours, ministering to him even to the foot of the Cross with the other Holy Women who did not, like the apostles, abandon him but proved to be faithful companions. I want to be associated with religious who will be called Faithful Companions of Jesus.

Holy Thursday 1820 is celebrated as the founding date of the Society. Marie Madeleine maintained her respect for the Jesuits and her commitment to Ignatian Spirituality, but also established a clear independence for her newly-found religious congregation. Sr Elizabeth Ryan, a former congregational leader, describes the humble beginning of the congregation in Amiens: 'She and the two young women who joined her began to teach some poor children to read, write and sew, as well as instructing them in the faith.' They were keen to enable the young women of the France of her time to be educated so that they would be able to take their place in the household and in society.

The first FCJ foundation in England was in Somers Town, London, where the Sisters took responsibility for an existing school. Other foundations of schools followed as the Sisters became known in London and in the north of England. The FCJ Sisters came to Oughterard, Co. Galway in 1842 through an invitation from the parish priest of the town, Dr Kirwan, who knew of the Sisters through his friend Fr Nerincks in Somers Town. A few years later the Sisters left Oughterard and in 1845, they established a secondary school in Limerick. Initially the Sisters held classes in a house at Richmond Place and later moved to Laurel Hill, where they were able to open a boarding and day school at post-primary level. Dean Cussen, Vicar General of the Diocese and a fluent French speaker, invited the FCJ Sisters to take responsibility for primary and secondary education in Bruff, Co. Limerick, where they remained for over a century (1856–2012).

Before Marie Madeleine's death in 1858, there were twelve foundations of this new congregation in France, ten in England, three in Ireland, two in Switzerland, one in Sardinia and one in Italy. In 1861, Fr Parle, a curate in Bunclody, then called Newtownbarry, invited the Sisters to provide a much needed education for the children of the parish. Initially the Sisters were involved at primary level but soon opened a secondary school as well as a boarding school for the education of girls in the south Leinster area. *San bhliain 1935, nuair a bhí an Rialtas ag déanamh iarracht ár dteanga dúchais a fhorbairt, bunaíodh Laurel Hill Coláiste FCJ.* The Coláiste continues to provide second level education through the medium of the Irish Language. September 2009 marked the beginning of a new era for the three FCJ Secondary Schools as they entered the Le Chéile Schools Trust.

Today, inspired by the Gospels and true to Marie Madeleine's founding ideals, companionship is evident as FCJ school communities work together in an atmosphere of support and love. This distinctiveness comes not from the education itself but from the spirit in which education is given. The climate of the school is not formed by the structure of the school or the curriculum but from the witness value of the people in the school. 'Courage and confidence' was a blessing dear to Marie Madeleine's heart as it reflected the peace which Jesus gave to his disciples. Discouragement has no place in an FCJ school; hope empowers us to fulfil our aspirations and grow towards spiritual, intellectual, social and emotional maturity. It is of the essence that the dignity of each person is recognised, as that of a human being made in the image of God. Respect for each person demands that when challenging situations arise, we seek dignified solutions for all concerned.

Following in the Ignatian tradition of a desire to 'find God in all things' and that all is 'for the greater glory of God', the pursuit of excellence, both personal and academic, is an inclusive value as students strive to achieve their personal best and become what they aspire to be in life. Inspired by the women at the foot of the cross, the unique giftedness of every student is recognised, nourished and celebrated. The school communities try to support each other in times of sorrow with loving respect while entering into joy and celebration in the same spirit. As Marie Madeleine wished, formation in faith is an expectation in FCJ schools. Relying on God's grace which enables each one to grow, the hope is that the students' faith will be nourished during their school years and become their life-giving force as they face into the future. The whole ethos of FCJ education is marked by gentleness, the gentle strength which is born of self-understanding and always keeps our hearts within the boundaries of justice, reason and love.

Frances Threadgold, school principal in FCJ Secondary School, Bunclody, Co. Wexford, describes how the original value of companionship is alive in the school: 'The companionship with

Jesus and others – that is the absolute central part of our school community. A simple example of how that companionship is lived out is – a team approach in everything we do.'

Strong in Companionship with Jesus and with each other we work together in the service of the Church to build the body of Christ.

(Above, all we are Companions of Jesus whose lives must reveal Him to the world.)

In Ireland the Faithful Companions of Jesus/
Le Chéile schools are:

- FCJ Secondary School, Bunclody, Co. Wexford
- Laurel Hill Coláiste FCJ, Limerick
- Laurel Hill Secondary School FCJ, Limerick

THE RELIGIOUS OF JESUS AND MARY

A tearful young French girl stood at the side of a main street in Lyon and watched in horror as her two brothers were dragged to their execution. Her tears were not seen nor her protests heard by the executioners. But her brothers did see her and eventually managed to communicate with her. 'Forgive Glady,' they said, 'as we forgive.'

Claudine Thévenet was born in Lyon in March 1774, the second of a family of seven children. 'Glady', as she was affectionately known had a warm and loving relationship with her brothers and sisters. Her father was a wealthy silk merchant and the family was deeply religious. At the age of nine Claudine was placed with the Benedictine nuns in St Peter's Abbey, Place des Terreaux. It was here that she received a strong intellectual and spiritual formation.

The French Revolution broke out when she was fifteen years of age. Claudine's elder brothers joined the anti-Revolutionary forces. The last of the fighting before the Revolutionary forces captured Lyon was tough and bitter. It took place close to the Thévenet home. The Revolutionary government in Paris ordered a brutal repression in Lyon as an example, and so those who had fought against the Revolution were to be executed. When the fighting ended Claudine went to look for her brothers amongst the dead but could not find them. Eventually she reached them in time to witness their execution, and to hear their final words: 'Forgive Glady, as we forgive.' These words would inspire Claudine for the rest of her life, although the shock of seeing the brutality of her brothers' death, and that of her uncle, gravely affected her. In later years Claudine would remember her brothers' message as she founded a new congregation to be called the Religious of Jesus and Mary. The gift of forgiveness was a core value in the many ministries for the poor in which she engaged as a young adult.

Following the horrific experience of her brothers' death, Claudine became active in the care and education of the poor. In 1815 she established a refuge for poor children called 'Providence of the Sacred Heart', taking charge of the many orphans who were abandoned after the Revolution. As a lay-woman, she worked for a number of years in the St Bruno Church in Lyon. Abbé Andre Coindre, her spiritual director, urged her to consider gathering her lay companions into a religious community. She did not wish to do that but Abbé Coindre eventually persuaded her to form a stable organisation with a precise and well-adapted set of rules. He drew up a plan based on the Rule of St Augustine and the Constitutions of St Ignatius of Loyola. On the feast of St Ignatius, 1818, she agreed to his urging and the congregation of the Religious of Jesus and Mary was founded on the hill slope of Fourvière. Claudine and her companions educated the poor young girls of the area, and with her family background of silk-weaving, she trained them in this specialist work too. Later she was asked to educate the children of wealthy families too and the income from this work enabled her to continue caring for poor children.

One of the earliest challenges for the new congregation was the objections of the weavers of Lyon to the success of the silk-weaving training which she was providing so expertly. Because of their orchestrated opposition, she had to abandon that aspect of work and concentrate totally on traditional education. Sr Mary Mulrooney, a congregational leader, emphasised the founding mission: 'Education was really our founding mission, to make Jesus and Mary known and loved in every social milieu, an education in faith and education for life.' Claudine and her lay associates had chosen the name 'The Association of the Sacred Hearts of Jesus and Mary' and when a religious congregation was founded, the name 'Religious of Jesus and Mary' was deemed appropriate. Claudine noted that the daughters of well-to-do families needed religious schooling as well as the daughters of poor families. She opened a boarding school for these young girls.

Four years after the beginning of the new congregation Abbé Coindre was transferred to Monistrol in the diocese of Puy. At his request Claudine, now known as Mother Marie Saint Ignatius, sent Sisters to work there with him. The congregation, in the following years, made many foundations outside France. Claudine died in 1837.

The question of opening a Convent of Jesus and Mary in Ireland had been discussed on a number of occasions by members of the congregation, but the French congregational leaders believed that they were not needed in Ireland, their aim being to send Sisters to missionary countries. However when an English Reverend Mother General, Mother St Clare, was elected in 1903, she decided that the congregation should send Sisters to Ireland. Dr Naughton, the Bishop of Killala at that time was a personal friend of one McCauley family whose daughters were educated by the Sisters in England. Two of the McCauley girls had entered the congregation in France. In 1912 the bishop welcomed the Sisters to the shores of Lough Conn, Co. Mayo, and by 1919 Gortnor Abbey there had both boarders and day pupils. In 1940 the Enniscrone school was opened, and nine years later the Irish Province of the congregation was established. The Sisters had inherited from Claudine a clear value for the school as a way of educating girls in their faith, and of educating them to take their rightful place in society.

Committed to the apostolic call and style of St Claudine Thévenet we serve in various educational, pastoral, social and spiritual ministries, through which we make known God's goodness and forgiving love, as revealed in the hearts of Jesus and Mary.

IN IRELAND THE RELIGIOUS OF JESUS AND MARY /
LE CHÉILE SCHOOLS ARE:

- Jesus and Mary Secondary School, Enniscrone, Co. Sligo.

- Jesus and Mary Secondary School, Gortnor Abbey, Cross-molina, Co. Mayo.

- Jesus and Mary Secondary School, Salerno, Salthill, Galway.

- Jesus and Mary College, Our Lady's Grove, Goatstown, Dublin.

THE RELIGIOUS OF CHRISTIAN EDUCATION

Once again the traumatic and all-embracing impact of the eighteenth-century French Revolution is the background for the story of another new religious congregation, the Religious of Christian Education. Post-Revolution France was 'in chaos'.

It was a difficult time for both Church and State and there was total confusion in the education system. Louis XIV's edict to have schools in each parish had been revoked, teachers were demoralised, and surviving schools provided only for boys. The new congregation, the Religious of Christian Education was founded within this period, in 1817 by the Abbé Louis Lafosse.

Louis Lafosse was born in 1772, lived through the Revolution and then began his studies for the priesthood. The anti-Church policy requiring an oath of allegiance to the State had to be faced by each newly-ordained priest. Louis Lafosse took the oath of allegiance, choosing not to be a fugitive priest in his own country. Later he repented of this and went on pilgrimage to his bishop who was living in exile in Germany for forgiveness.

On his return to Echaufour in France he was deeply moved by how people were affected by post-Revolution poverty and misery. He decided that the most immediate need which he could address was the education of girls. With four young women, led by Marie-Anne Dutertre, Fr Lafosse founded the new congregation on 21 November 1817, in Échauffour, Normandy. Marie-Anne Dutertre and her companions were educated, zealous and committed local young women. They became the first members of the new congregation. Fr Lafosse, with these early Sisters, developed a vision which was to provide the girls of the Echaufour region with a solid education, which was both human and Christian. One of the Sisters stresses how gifted and skilled Père Lafosse was as an educator: he had a wonderful methodology of teaching, which was admired greatly, and people would write to him and ask 'how did you do it', and 'what did you use', 'what method'?

The congregation was formally approved in 1821. The Sisters quickly established communities throughout Normandy and the neighbouring regions of France and Belgium.

The schools of the new congregation were highly respected. They were asked by local authorities to found a training college for teachers so that more schools could benefit within the Lafosse tradition of teaching.

The Sisters, however, were still living within a State-supported anti-religious culture. They could not be seen publicly as religious and they could not own the properties in which they lived and worked. Despite these constraints they continued with their educational mission. These difficult French laws along with interesting English connections, led the Sisters to develop their mission in England in 1898. A number of English Catholic girls had been sent to the Religious of Christian Education schools in France, and English army personnel, whose daughters had been educated by the Sisters in France, suggested that they come to Farnborough near the army base in Aldershot. Moving to England, the Sisters could be recognised as religious and could own property.

When founding new schools and providing training for teachers, Fr Lafosse stressed that the young people were to be educated according to their abilities, and that teachers had the responsibility to discover and foster the talents of their students. The schools were to create a learning environment, a 'family spirit' in which this could happen. Many of the Sisters received government recognition for their contribution to education at national level. From the start, the Sisters awakened the social conscience of the students, making them aware of justice issues and what they could do about them.

The motivation for students was summed up as: 'Make the world a better place for your being in it.'

Many of the Religious of Christian Education living and working in England were originally from Ireland so, as one of the Sisters said: 'It was always a desire of the Sisters to come to Ireland.' Charles McQuaid, then Archbishop of Dublin, invited the Sisters to provide a school in Dublin. Our Lady's School in Terenure opened in 1953, and two years later a boarding school in Rathnew, Co. Wicklow was founded.

Faith formation, the 'family spirit' and model of education created by Pére Lafosse were core values for the schools. Parents' committees were set up and students' councils became a reality long before they were nationally accepted. Faith formation was a central value. A school principal speaks about these values being present in the contemporary school: 'These values, that Fr Lafosse promoted, are lived in the school; the students also have a sense of belonging as they are learning, and the ability to reflect on all the experiences of school life.'

Following the ideals of Fr Lafosse and the early Sisters, the school is a community which stands for Christian values. The Education offered aims at a search for the Truth, the formation of Christian Faith and the growth and personal development of each person.

In Ireland the Religious of Christian Education / Le Chéile school is:

- Our Lady's School, Templeogue, Dublin.

THE URSULINE SISTERS

The story of the founder of the Ursuline Sisters might be titled 'The Woman Who said No to the Pope'! In 1540 during a visit to Rome Angela Merici did actually decline Pope Clement VII's invitation to remain there to develop her pastoral and educational work. Having made this decision she returned to her home at Brescia, Italy.

Angela Merici was born in the old part of Desenzano on Lake Garda in northern Italy between 1470–5. The daughter of Giovanni Merici, a farmer, and a member of the highly-respected Biancosi family, she had several siblings. With them she helped in the home and family farm. Her early life was influenced by the faith of her parents. Her parents were spiritual and well-informed people, and Angela received her initial education and spiritual training from them.

Sorrow soon ended a happy childhood when Angela's parents and one of her sisters died. She went to live with an uncle in the neighboring town of Salo. Though in the midst of the Renaissance with its renewal in learning, art and culture, she began to withdraw more into a reflective and spiritual way of living. Angela, a teenager, realised that she wanted to do something worthwhile with her life. She was irresistibly drawn to doing more and, despite opposition from her adopted family, she joined the Franciscan Third Order. This was to be a turning point in her development. The spirituality and mission of St Francis were to become key factors in her decisions, with pilgrimages being one aspect of this spirituality. She made difficult journeys to both the Holy Land and to Rome.

In 1516, when she was about forty years of age, Angela travelled to Brescia. The city was recovering from a devastating French invasion. Church and faith as well as the intellectual and economic life of the city were in need of reform. In Brescia she met with a reform group of lay people, a brotherhood which established infirmaries for the ill, and encouraged a religious renewal among the laity. Women joined the group and they provided care for widows and girls. She emphasised the dignity bestowed upon each individual and was gentle and respectful in all her relationships. Within a few years of meeting with this group of lay people she became their spiritual advisor and leader. The driving force in Angela's life was her personal relationship with God.

With some of these companions she made the journey to Rome where she had a special meeting with Pope Clement VII, and during which she had to discern the papal invitation to remain in Rome. Brescia to which Angela returned had once been a flourishing city full of intellectual life and the benefits of the Renaissance. When Angela first came to live there in 1516 she found a city scarred by the ravages of war and intellectual decay. Its citizens had risen in rebellion against French invaders and were defeated. Official religion was in decay. Bishops seldom visited their dioceses, and many priests and religious were living immoral lives. For the very first time she encountered the devastation caused by war and immorality.

Despite her age and failing health Angela began to develop a new community of women in 1531. In 1535, the Company of St Ursula was formed. This was a religious community of women which was fundamentally different in its self-concept from other congregations existing then. She called the new group the Company of St Ursula. The company combined open-mindedness and religious commitment in a way which opened up new possibilities for women. The first Sisters did not live in convents, but remained integrated in their families or stayed at their work places. Angela chose St Ursula as patron saint because she saw the saint as a model for women and a patron for learning and courage. Angela believed that women, specifically in their roles within their families, were critical to the transformation of society. Thus the education of young girls and women developed as one of the Company's primary works.

After Angela's time the Ursuline Company evolved into a religious congregation becoming one of the first female teaching congregations making a major impact on the religious education of young people in Europe and the New World. Today, more than 470 years later, the formation of strong, dynamic, well-educated women continues as one of the Ursulines' primary objectives.

Ursuline links with Ireland date back to the early-seventeenth century. Francis Kirwan, an Irish man who was ordained a priest and consecrated as bishop in exile, met the Ursulines in Caen in northern France. His purpose was to have Irish girls receive a Catholic education there. In 1647 other Irish bishops asked the Sisters to found a convent in Ireland. However, plans for such a venture in Galway were overtaken by the Cromwellian invasion. Bishop Kirwan was imprisoned but later he reached Caen where the Sisters welcomed him.

The Ursulines eventually arrived in Ireland in 1771 thanks to Nano Nagle, the founder of the Irish Presentation Sisters. Margaret Butler, a cousin of Nano's, had become an Ursuline in France, being professed there at the age of forty-seven. Early in 1767 Nano joined her to be initiated into religious life and to learn French. She wanted to pursue the idea of an Ursuline foundation in Ireland. With permission from the Archbishop of Paris, Margaret and Nano travelled to Le Havre and boarded a ship for Cork. Nano had property in Cork where she was willing to provide for an Ursuline convent but Margaret's health failed and after one year she returned to France. Nano continued with her work of providing schools. With money left by her uncle, and with help from her brother, Nano built a convent in Cove Lane, Cork, waiting for Ursuline Sisters to arrive. In April 1771 the first group arrived in Cork. They opened a boarding school in January of the following year, one of the first Irish Catholic secondary schools for girls. Irish Ursuline convents and schools grew in number and prospered.

There is only one mission, the mission of Jesus. Anointed by the Spirit, he was sent to bring the Good News of God's unconditional love.

In Ireland Ursuline/Le Chéile schools are:

- Ursuline Secondary School, Blackrock, Cork.
- Ursuline Secondary School, Thurles, Co. Tipperary.
- St Angela's School, Ursuline Convent, Waterford.
- Ursuline College, Finisklin, Sligo.
- St Angela's College, Patrick's Hill, Cork.

Weaving the Le Chéile Threads

The Le Chéile Trust and the Le Chéile schools have inherited the founding stories, the heritage in these stories and, most importantly, they have inherited the charisms of the religious congregations. They are now blessings for Le Chéile. Individual stories, many in different countries, all in different times come together as the Le Chéile founding story. Each story reflects God's loving plan.

Dominic de Guzmán, Angela de Merici, John Baptist de La Salle, Daniel Delaney, Louis Bautain, Victoire de Begny, Claudine Thévenet, Anne Janouvey, Louis Lafosse, Elizabeth Prout, Frances Taylor, Margaret Aylward and Cornelia Peacock share their lives and their faith with us, the members of the Le Chéile Community of Schools.

This community of schools, the Le Chéile Schools Trust, was founded in 2009 when the members of each of the congregations recognised a need in their time – the need to ensure that the schools so courageously founded in past centuries could continue in Ireland in the future. That is why the story continues, and the inherited spirituality is a Le Chéile spirituality for our time.

TOWARDS A SPIRITUALITY FOR LE CHÉILE SCHOOLS

It is unlikely that an announcement in the summer of 2012 from the Department of Education and Skills regarding the patronage of fourteen new schools was considered by many in Ireland as having a place in the unfolding story of the founders. However for everyone involved in Le Chéile there was no doubt that it heralded the next phase of the relatively new story of the coming together of the Le Chéile congregations. The Minister for Education and Skills, Ruairi Quinn, announced that the Le Chéile Schools Trust had been awarded the patronage of the first new Catholic post-primary voluntary secondary school to be built in over twenty years. It would be situated in west Dublin, opening in 2014 to cater for the growing population of the Tyrrelstown area. This government decision was made after a tendering process in which the Le Chéile Trust had demonstrated that there were was a high level of interest among local parents in having a school that would reflect the values and educational vision of the Trust in their area. This exciting development in the early days of the Trust may be seen as vindication of the work of the congregations whose stated aims in founding Le Chéile were:

- To affirm their commitment to the future of Catholic Education;

- To provide for the needs of the students and communities in their schools;

- To honour their partnership with the government in the education system.

(Le Chéile Charter, p. 1)

While the Trust was established primarily with a view to maintaining the schools already open, now within four years of its establishment the passion and vision at the heart of the stories of the founders is to find expression in a new school that will embody the shared story that is Le Chéile. It will not be a school like the others in the Trust where a particular heritage dominates. Rather it will be one that will model what the coming together of the stories means for a twenty-first century Catholic school in Ireland and in that way will indicate for all our schools the great richness of tradition in which each and every one of them shares.

In order to understand what this means for the sixty-one schools in practice we wish to devote this final section of our book to weaving together three further threads into this rich tapestry. Firstly, even though it may be self-evident there is a need for future generations to reflect on the fact that there would be no founders if it were not for Jesus and his proclamation of the Good News. Reflecting on his story and how we understand it leads us on to two key ideas that allow us to make a vibrant and dynamic connection between the Gospel, the founders and our schools today. These key ideas are: Charism and Spirituality.

JESUS AND THE KINGDOM OF GOD

Deep faith in and devotion to the person of Jesus represent the most important shared facts about the lives of the women and men who founded the congregations in Le Chéile. Even though they may have lived in different centuries, in different countries and dealt with very different contexts, they all viewed the world through the lens of Christian faith. This faith was nourished through their belonging to the Church, through prayer and a love of the Scriptures which brought them to an awareness of Jesus not as a historical figure from the past but as the risen Lord whose Spirit continues to breathe life into the world. They all came to an appreciation of just how good the Good News of the Kingdom is and each of them in turn found ways to put flesh on the values they found in the Gospel story.

If we consider that a major part of Jesus' relatively short public life was given over to teaching then a good place to start would be to reflect on what he taught and how. The content of his first lesson was short and somewhat enigmatic: 'The Kingdom of God has come near; repent and believe the Good News' (Mark 1:15). From the outset the Good News is linked to Jesus' proclamation of the Kingdom. Most Christians are familiar with the Kingdom idea through praying the Our Father and asking that God's Kingdom come. When questioned about what that might mean or what they are praying for many people relate it to the idea of heaven and the hope of eternal life. However this is a very restricted view and fails to take into account the many and varied ways in which Jesus spoke about it. The clue to its meaning lies in the second half of the petition in the prayer that Jesus taught: 'Thy will be done on earth as it is in heaven.' The Kingdom is, put simply, a metaphor for God's will; in other words what God wants for us and for the world; it is about how people should engage with the experience of human living. Jesus as a revealer of God's will embodies and demonstrates the mind of God when it comes to how we should engage with being human.

Gospel Values and the Parables of Jesus

Jesus never offered a definition of the kingdom that he proclaimed but rather he opted to demonstrate what it meant by the stories he told and the work that he did. His teaching is offered through parables and these have been usefully defined as short stories with a double meaning. The parables of Jesus reflected his world; the village life of farmers, shepherds and fishermen. They featured families divided and kings throwing banquets, people struggling with debt while others rejoice because they find a treasure beyond price, or a coin they thought they had lost; unbelievable harvests and great catches of fish along with doubts about the fruitfulness of the land. In terms of content they are not particularly religious, they don't feature holy men and women saying their prayers or giving sermons. Using the here and now these stories highlight attitudes and behaviour that reveal the presence or indeed absence of God and his way of responding to the world of human experience. In short they highlight the values of the Kingdom, which we also call gospel values.

Two of the better known parables, the Good Samaritan and the Prodigal Son illustrate this point very well. However they suffer a little from being too well known to the extent that the strong message of each of these stories is sometimes diluted when they are read out of context and merely taken as moral instruction.

The Good Samaritan is often thought to be a story that teaches us to be good to people in need. However when read in its context in the Gospel of Luke (10:25–37) it becomes clear that it is much more about challenging a mindset that seeks to set limits on who is worthy or deserving of our compassion. By choosing to make a Samaritan the hero Jesus has already laid down a marker and irritated the lawyer who asked the question 'who is my neighbour?' On religious and political grounds the lawyer would hold Samaritans in contempt and yet the message of the story is: go and behave like the Samaritan – be willing to learn, from someone you despise, that your world view is too small and that your mind is closed. It is easy to see how being good to people in need is a gospel value, however the story is equally and perhaps even more about recognising your prejudices and leaving them behind – that too is a gospel value.

The story of the Prodigal Son is probably the best known parable of them all and is usually thought to be a story to help people understand that God will always forgive them. So we know from this and other examples of the teaching of Jesus that forgiveness is a gospel value. However the context in which the story is told and the punchline that completes it serve as a reminder that this parable is also about challenging a mindset. The context for the parables in Luke 15 is given at the beginning of the chapter:

> Now all the tax collectors and sinners were coming near to listen to
> him and the Pharisees and the scribes were grumbling and saying
> this fellow welcomes sinners and eats with them. So he told *them*
> this parable (Lk 15:1–3).

The story of The Prodigal Son is preceded by two parables that
focus on the attitude of God towards the sinner. The Lost Sheep and
the Lost Coin present God as the irresponsible shepherd who is
willing to risk everything to go after the one lost sheep or as the
woman who will not stop searching until she finds the lost coin. In
both cases there is unbounded joy at the outcome when what was
lost is found. That format is followed in the story of the two sons.
The focus this time is not only the attitude of God as the father in
the story but also and perhaps more significantly from the listener's
point of view, the attitude of the older brother.

He is outraged and appalled at the extent of the father's
indulgence of the brat who showed a complete disregard for
everything they hold dear as a family. By any human reckoning the
older brother deserves our sympathy – the father's response to the
younger son is unreasonable and even hurtful. So in this story there
are two outcomes. We see the unbounded joy of the father who
wants to throw a party and the righteous indignation of the dutiful
brother who wants to have nothing to do with this farce. What
gospel value is being promoted here? In theory everybody likes the
idea of forgiveness but in practice we make up our minds about
who is deserving and who is not. So we are invited to recognise the
extent to which we are like the Pharisees and scribes who complain
that Jesus welcomes the wrong kind of people, and to open
ourselves to the God who calls us to a more radical understanding
of love.

Both these parables highlight the problem we have in coming to
terms with a God whose gracious generosity is never earned but is
always given. The same message is present in the parable of the
vineyard workers in Matthew 20:1–16. Taken at face value this story
seems to suggest that an employer can do whatever he likes and
ignore the demands of basic justice when it comes to paying his
workers. Once again the context of the proclamation of the kingdom

offers the clue to its real meaning which focuses on God's desire to draw all people to himself without distinction. Clearly this deliberately provocative story turns human reasoning on its head as Jesus explains to his hearers that their idea of God is little more than a projection of their restricted world view that rests solely on the idea of merit and one which fails completely to understand that the Father of Jesus whose 'kingdom' he proclaims can only be understood in terms of unconditional love and compassion.

Gospel Values and the Actions of Jesus

If the stories Jesus told give us an insight into this Kingdom he proclaims then so do his actions. The decision to sit at a table with those designated as 'tax collectors and sinners' caused offense because by this action he welcomes those who are excluded and in the process puts himself on the outside (Mark 2:13–17). His action is calculated to demonstrate something about the nature of the God whom Jesus serves, the one who actively seeks out the lost and this is also true of his healing ministry. The miracles are sometimes thought of as proof that Jesus was who he said he was – the son of God. Such a reading fails to take into account how his actions are connected to his preaching of God's Kingdom. They are not performed in order to show power or to win over followers but rather they are indicators of the kind of healing God wants to bring to a broken humanity. Healing a leper (Mark 1:40–45), a woman suffering a haemorrhage (Mark 5:24–34), or another woman crippled for eighteen years (Lk 14:10–17) were actions that had consequences. Those healed now find themselves able to take their place in their communities from which to a greater or lesser extent they had been excluded because of their condition. However this healing ministry also offended others whose idea of God had much more to do with the exercise of power and keeping social and religious outcasts in their place. The evidence for this is to be seen in the story of the crippled woman in the synagogue who is healed on the Sabbath. In this instance the healing takes place in a context that highlights how the practice of religion may work as an oppressive force. As a woman this person is already disadvantaged in the synagogue liturgy. Women could attend but were in a separate gallery at the back. As a women suffering from an illness she was doubly marginalised. Her ailment was considered as a punishment for sin. Jesus' response to her challenges the religious perspective of the leader of the assembly whose mindset is revealed when he protests at what is taking place. This dynamic of challenging a certain type of religiosity is also at work in the story of the man with the withered hand (Mark 3:1–6). The extent to which this is deemed to be subversive behaviour is evident in the fact that the story ends with the religious and political leaders joining forces to destroy Jesus. The values of the Kingdom present in Jesus' ministry in these stories are those of compassion and justice and they rest entirely on awareness that the God whom Jesus reveals is concerned with the well-being (salvation!) of every human being. Just as the parables challenge our mindsets so does the healing work of Jesus.

GOSPEL VALUES AND THE CHRISTIAN COMMUNITY

The focus so far has been on the words and deeds of Jesus as the basis for an understanding of gospel values. However, the early church proclaimed the person of Jesus, the crucified and risen Christ, as well as his message. Their new found faith was not primarily about a new ethic but about a relationship with a person. Baptism was viewed as an entry into his life and a new relationship with God made possible through the gift of the Holy Spirit. This new life had consequences for believers as they witnessed to it by their lives which were to be in conformity with that of Jesus. The letters of Paul are the earliest documents of the church and in them Paul typically begins by addressing the particular problems of the community he is writing to and then moves on to exhort them to behave in ways that are consistent with their beliefs about Jesus. A very good illustration of what this means can be seen in the final section of the letter to the Romans where Paul exhorts a community that has experienced tension between the Jewish and Gentile sections of that community to live out the consequences of their new found faith.

Let love be genuine; hate what is evil, hold fast to what is good;
love one another with mutual affection; outdo one another in
showing honour.
Do not lag in zeal, be ardent in spirit, serve the Lord.
Rejoice in hope, be patient in suffering, persevere in prayer.
Contribute to the needs of the saints; extend hospitality to strangers.
Bless those who persecute you; bless and do not curse them.
Rejoice with those who rejoice, weep with those who weep.
Live in harmony with one another; do not be haughty, but associate
with the lowly; do not claim to be wiser than you are.
Do not repay anyone evil for evil, but take thought for what is noble
in the sight of all. If it is possible, so far as it depends on you,
live peaceably with all (Romans 12:9–18).

He is not offering them a rule book and he never uses the phrase 'gospel values'. However here and elsewhere in his letters he makes it clear that being a Christian is not so much about creating a list of things to do as developing attitudes and behaviour that ought to characterise the life of the community. The values they live by flow from their understanding of Christ and their relationship with him. There are other key passages from Paul that illustrate the point as he exhorts communities not just to keep a set of commandments but to embrace a world view, a mindset in which human living is seen as a grateful response to the compassionate God who is made known to them through the Goods News of the Kingdom (1 Cor 13:1–13, Gal 5:22–26, Eph 4:1–6, Phil 4:4–9).

Even this brief overview of the founding story of Christianity from the New Testament makes it clear that the Good News that Jesus proclaims, once it is heard and believed leads to a personal transformation and to a new way of living that is rooted in gospel values. These 'values' transcend mere good manners. They are rooted in the infinite worth of each person as a child of God. They call us to model our attitudes and behaviour on the words and deeds of Jesus. This is precisely what was taking place in the lives of the Le Chéile founders as they recognised how the work of education was an invaluable way to help children to come to an awareness of their unique dignity and worth. It is no coincidence that each of the founders recognised that the gift they were sharing would be reliant on a community of like-minded people who were motivated by the same vision working together to give concrete expression to the gift. In the process of being faithful to the Good News each founder was, along with the companions they gathered around them, sharing a gift that was making present the Kingdom of God proclaimed by Jesus. What was that gift? Let us turn to consider that now.

Charism

In Ireland the work of education takes place within the legal framework of the Education Act 1998. This means that we are in the interesting position of having legislation that recognises the value of the 'founding intention' of the school and the importance of maintaining its 'characteristic spirit'. This is precisely where we find the link between the stories we have read and the reason for the existence of the Le Chéile Trust. That link between the life stories of the founders and our schools as they operate today can be summed up in the very important word, '*charism*'.

At the outset it is worth pointing out that charism is not to be identified with charisma which in our time and in ordinary conversation is a more widely used word. Charisma usually refers to certain qualities that an individual may possess that would mark him or her out as a gifted leader, someone who will inspire others to follow a certain path or to commit to a particular cause. However when we speak of charism we are not limiting ourselves to a focus on the particular qualities of a given founder we are considering rather a concept that lies at the heart of what Christians believe about God.

The word charism has its roots in the Greek word *charis*. It is found in the New Testament some 156 times and it is frequently translated by the word grace or gift, but one dictionary of New Testament Greek suggests a range of meanings including 'a special manifestation of the divine presence, power, glory, favour or blessing'. Underlying its use in the source documents of Christianity is the idea of God as the source of every grace or gift. Jesus in his life and ministry is the embodiment of this gift. His works of teaching, healing, compassion and forgiveness are all expressions of the grace of God freely given and operative among us. They are a witness to the reality of what Jesus calls the Kingdom of God which we have described as God's will for the world. John affirms in his gospel that Jesus is the Word of God made flesh and that through him we have received 'grace upon grace' (John 1:14). Part of our difficulty today when it comes to speaking of this is a linguistic or semantic one. For many, the language of grace is linked exclusively to the realm of piety. However for the writers of the New Testament this gift is what makes it possible for us to live a fully human life (John 10:10). We are made fully alive when we catch a glimpse of how much we are loved – this is the gift of God in Christ, it is the Good News, this is the original charism! Amazing as this insight is, it is enhanced in the New Testament by the realisation that through the Holy Spirit (which is the Spirit of Jesus) that is given to the believer we not only receive the gift, we become bearers of it to others. St Paul puts it this way: 'The love of God has been poured into our hearts by the Holy Spirit that we have received'(Romans 5:5). For Paul this means that baptism, through which we receive the Holy Spirit, is a call to share in the mission and ministry of Jesus, to share in his charism – to become a witness to the compassion of God. Writing to the young Christian community in Corinth, Paul summed it up in this way:

> Now there are a variety of gifts but the same Spirit; and there are a variety of services, but the same Lord; and there are a variety of activities but it is the same God who activates all of them in everyone. To each is given the manifestation of the Spirit for the common good (1 Cor 12:4–7).

It is not surprising therefore that the word *charis* in the New Testament is often linked to an inner power or strength (Acts 4:33, 6:33). The gift empowers the believer to undertake the task, to accomplish the mission, aware that he or she is involved in something that transcends the self and points always towards the Kingdom. 'Like good stewards of the manifold grace of God, serve one another with whatever gift each of you has received' (1 Pet

4:10). In the Scriptures Jesus is not described as one who came to tell us what to do, he does not seek to impose a new morality – rather he came to tell us who we are in God and to invite us, indeed to challenge us to live out of that giftedness.

Throughout its history the Church has recognised that the fundamental gift – the Holy Spirit – has been at work in the lives of particular people and in the ministries of particular religious congregations. The charism of each of the congregations involves a particular call to faith. It is a way of reading and responding to Christ in a particular time and place. In the stories of the founders that we have touched upon this is precisely what was unfolding as they journeyed through life. They were not seated in ivory towers removed from reality but were immersed in the world of their time, its pain, its problems and its opportunities. Their charism involved a particular experience and expression of the gift of Christ who embodies the effective love of God in the world. This understanding of *charism* means that it is not just about specific individuals and the way they responded in faith. It emphasises that the effect of their witness is also a gift to the Church, a gift that has been nurtured by the community life and spirituality of the congregation. That is how we have come to know it and to share in it. It is not at all unusual to hear past pupils or teachers who have worked in a particular congregational school speaking about its character, that spirit or atmosphere that pervades the work of education there. This quality which can be hard to define is sometimes described by the word *ethos* but in the Catholic tradition there has always been a recognition that this quality is a gift – a gift of the Holy Spirit through the congregation to the Church and society.

This brings us to our time and to the Le Chéile Trust, to our schools and our work in education. We are not living in revolutionary France, or through the industrial revolution in England or even in post-Catholic emancipation Ireland. We are living in a secular Ireland enduring its worst economic crisis since the founding of the State, an Ireland in which the Church as an institution has been damaged by scandals and has lost much of its authority, and an Ireland that is more ethnically and religiously diverse than it has ever been. On a broader scale we are living in an era when ecology is becoming the issue of our time, when the economies of Asia are becoming the dominant players in world markets and when religious belief is under pressure from an aggressive secularism on the one hand and fundamentalism on the other. This is the context in which we talk about charism and Catholic education. In the creation of the Le Chéile Trust the congregations recognise that their charism is not only theirs – it is a gift of God to the Church and to the world and in the spirit of their founders they wish to continue sharing that gift as they have exercised it in and through the ministry of education. Each community in the congregations shared in a very direct way in the mission of education that defined the work of the congregation. In the *Le Chéile Charter* the core values derived from the gospel and expressed in the charisms of each order are stated for our time and what that might mean to us is stated very clearly in that charter:

> A key challenge for the future is to develop a vision of how the charism of baptism and the charism associated with the founding congregations can be integrated in a future that will be based predominantly on a lay spirituality (p. 9).

Why is that a key challenge? Principally it is asking the school communities to recognise that the same Spirit that moved Jesus to proclaim the Kingdom of God and Paul to found Christian communities, the Spirit that inspired the founders to do what they did in their time is moving us to respond in our time and in our way. We share that Spirit and we are asked to trust that Pentecost is not a yesterday event but rather something that occurs again and again in every era. This brings us to the next key element in the Le Chéile story: Spirituality.

Spirituality

This is a widely-used word with a whole host of definitions. However the context of the emergence of the Le Chéile Schools Trust invites us to think of spirituality in terms of how we give expression to the value system and beliefs that we embrace and that inform our work in education. Given that the Le Chéile Trust has arisen out of a collaborative effort on the part of the congregations to share the gospel values they have derived from their founding stories we know where to go to work out a spirituality that will inform the daily life of our schools. Following the example of the founders we look to the life of Jesus who came that we might have life in its fullness.

In the first part of this book the telling of the stories of the founders is the way into understanding the heritage of the congregations. This is a vital aspect of the Le Chéile vision which seeks not only to maintain the congregational heritage but also to share them. This explains why in the Charter of the Le Chéile Trust each of the congregations has written a heritage page that seeks to summarise their charism and the characteristic spirit of their schools. Reading these pages it quickly becomes apparent that 'the beautiful enterprise of education' goes way beyond the simple passing on of information. It is about transformation, the process enabling our students to become fully alive human beings. As the Charter states: 'Transformative education is essentially a spiritual process.'

One way of helping us to reflect on that process is to focus on three key words that draw together the core elements of what we might call a Le Chéile spirituality:

WELCOME – WISDOM – WITNESS.

Reflection on these elements is for everyone in the school community: management, staff, pupils and parents.

WELCOME

A Le Chéile school will be a welcoming place and the basis for that welcome is the unique dignity and worth of each person who crosses the threshold. This openness is demonstrated for us in the gospel through the encounters that Jesus had with a very broad cross section of the people of his time. Many of those he received with open arms were on the edge of their society because of prejudice based on age, gender, ethnicity, social status or religion. Jesus surprised his contemporaries, including his disciples, by his willingness to engage with such people and to even invite them to become disciples and share in his mission. Similarly in the stories of the founders we repeatedly come across instances where they sought to welcome the poor, the illiterate and those who were victims of violence, injustice and social inequality. The purpose of the welcome was to empower them to take control of their lives through becoming aware of their dignity.

The task for the Le Chéile school today is to reflect on how this welcoming and inclusive attitude is experienced in the day-to-day running of the school. In a reflective context, boards of management, staff, student councils and parents associations can explore this aspect of the characteristic spirit of the school. Engaging in such a process will lead to an awareness that a welcoming school is also a place of compassion and forgiveness.

It is necessary to acknowledge and affirm where and how these values are found in the current practices and procedures of the school. It is also important to seek ways to ensure that they remain not simply words on a mission statement.

From a planning point of view this has implications for enrolment, code of behaviour and anti-bullying policies. While engaging in this process the school community is more likely to respond enthusiastically to a reflective evaluation if it is understood not simply as a statutory requirement but as a vitally important way of maintaining an open and hospitable atmosphere in school. Each individual has a role to play and a significant contribution to make in creating this spirit and in turn each person can benefit hugely from working in this caring environment.

WISDOM

In creating an atmosphere of welcome in the le Chéile school we are seeking to create a context in which teaching and learning can take place. We are engaged in the pursuit of wisdom, grateful that we have been gifted with reason and a hunger to understand and appreciate the world in which we live. From the beginning this has been at the heart of the Church's mission in education. Once again Jesus the teacher is our role model here. He invited those who came to hear him to reflect on their experience of life. He encouraged and comforted them in the face of hardships and difficulties but he was not afraid to challenge them to face up to their own shortcomings and to see things differently. This approach is once again very evident in the lives of the founders. Not one of them was interested in the pursuit of knowledge for its own sake but each in turn sought to enable their students to develop as human beings. Their concern, in a whole range of different contexts, was to assist their students, whether adults or children, to be aware of their skills and talents. Thus they were empowered to take their place in the world and to live well in it, contributing to the well-being of others. Given this perspective on education it is not surprising that the founders paid such attention to the training of teachers and were often pioneers in pedagogical method, challenging the accepted wisdom of their day in relation to such things as corporal punishment and promoting child-centred and caring approaches in the classroom.

The context of the Le Chéile school today presents some new challenges and others that have been around for a long time. The technological revolution has led some students to ask: Why do they need teachers when they've got Google? Other voices heard today in discussions on education are from those concerned primarily with the needs of the economy. Still others are focused on academic performance in league tables, whether national or international. What can easily be lost sight of in this debate is the importance of the learner and the various ways in which they learn. Central to that and more important than any other in-school factor relating to student achievement is the relationship between the student and the teacher. So in our schools as we reflect on teaching and learning our questions are informed by a wider understanding of education which also embraces the spiritual and religious dimension of human existence. School self-evaluation programmes are becoming the norm and this development can provide us with a very welcome opportunity to recognise good practice and to make changes where necessary so that the educational experience of the children across all areas of the curriculum can be improved and enhanced. However at the heart of the Le Chéile school is a desire 'to facilitate and support each student's search for truth and meaning. This is why we encourage them to strive for excellence in all areas of human growth' (*Le Chéile Charter*, p. 5). Ways and means of doing this are to be worked out in conjunction with the whole school community, always bearing in mind that we are not simply servants of the state or the economy. We are in the service of a broader and brighter vision that, while rooted in this world, reaches beyond it.

WITNESS

If the Le Chéile school is a welcoming place of care and compassion where the pursuit of wisdom is supported and celebrated then we are already engaged in this third core element of Catholic education. We are witnessing to a world view that recognises the worth and dignity of every person as made in the image and likeness of God. We are affirming the goodness and beauty of creation and seeking to protect the environment. We are working to promote social justice and peace both at home and abroad. This is a world view that derives from faith in the life, death and resurrection of Jesus Christ and has been passed on and developed by generations of faithful Christians throughout the long history of the Church. The founders of the Le Chéile congregations all witnessed to their faith by their using their God-given talents in the service of others. They drew inspiration and strength for that task through their lives of prayer and they sought to pass on to the students in their care a living faith that would offer them direction and hope in their lives. This was done not only by the marvellous example of their own lives but also by a commitment to prayer and religious education as core elements in the life of the school.

In an increasingly secular Ireland this is considered by some as a contentious area. Sensitivity to the people of other faiths and of no faith must be a part of the welcoming school, however we would not be true to the Catholic heritage of the founding congregations or to our characteristic spirit if we chose to abandon or downplay the value of religious education, or if we failed to celebrate faith by providing occasions of personal and communal prayer in the school. Positive experiences of worship at key moments in the liturgical year or at times of particular celebration or crisis offer students opportunities for spiritual growth that may richly complement the study of RE in the classroom setting. We must remember that faith can never be imposed and must always be by invitation and if the explicit religious witness given is not a reflection of the values that guide the day-to-day experience of the school then it may do more harm than good. That is why, with the founders, we seek to be authentic witnesses, aware of our limitations and always ready to ask for God's help in being faithful to our task.

An authentic spirituality does not emerge from the pages of a book. It can only be real if it is forged in the desire to give faithful expression to an inner life. These reflections on what a Le Chéile spirituality might look life are offered in the hope that by being faithful to the shared heritage we have received and reflecting on the challenges of the times in which we live we might continue to contribute richly to that core mission of the Church that is the education of the young.

THE LE CHÉILE PRAYER

In the power of the Spirit
and in keeping with the traditions of our founding Congregations
we pray that,
for students, parents and teachers alike;
our schools
may be places of learning and discovery
places of hope and joy
places of courage and confidence
places of gratitude and generosity
places of faith rooted in love.

We make this prayer through Christ our Lord. Amen.

The Le Chéile Litany

Dominic de Guzmán, searcher for the truth
    (The Dominicans)   *Pray for us*

Angela Merici, listener and pilgrim
    (The Ursulines)   *Pray for us*

John Baptist de La Salle, patron of teachers
    (The De La Salle Brothers)   *Pray for us*

Marie Madeliene D'Houët, companion of Jesus
    (Faithful Companions of Jesus)   *Pray for us*

Anne-Marie Javouhey, woman of courage
    (Sisters of St Joseph of Cluny)   *Pray for us*

Claudine Thévenet, woman of forgiveness
    (Religious of Jesus and Mary)   *Pray for us*

Daniel Delaney, caring pastor
    (The Patrician Brothers)   *Pray for us*

Louis Bautain, man of vision
    (Sisters of St Louis)   *Pray for us*

Louis Lafosse, man of integrity
    (Religious of Christian Education)   *Pray for us*

Margaret Aylward, woman of faith
    (Holy Faith Sisters)   *Pray for us*

Elizabeth Prout, friend of the poor
    (Cross and Passion Sisters)   *Pray for us*

Frances Taylor, compassionate guide
    (Poor Servants of the Mother of God)   *Pray for us*

Genevieve Dupuis, faithful disciple
    (Sisters of Charity of Saint Paul)   *Pray for us*

Cornelia Connelly, woman of hope
    (Sisters of the Holy Child Jesus)   *Pray for us*

SELECT BIBLIOGRAPHY

Bellito, C.M., *Church History 101: A Concise Overview*, 2008, Missouri: Ligouri, 2008.

Carleton, W., 'Traits and stories of the Irish peasantry,' (1843) in Hyland, Á., & Milne, K. (eds.), *Irish Educational Documents*, pp. 69–71, vol. I, Dublin: Church of Ireland College of Education, 1987.

Clancy, P., Drudy, S., Lynch, K., & O'Dowd, L. (eds.), *Irish Society, Sociological perspectives*, Dublin: Institute of Public Administration, pp. 467–95.

Claudine Thévenet (1774–1837). Virgin, founder of the Congregation of the Religious of Jesus and Mary. Retrieved from www.vatican.va/ newsservices/liturgy/saints/nslitdoc19930321theveneten.html.

Congregation for Catholic Education, *The Catholic School*, Dublin: Veritas, 1977.

Coolahan, J., *Irish Education History and Structure*, Dublin: Institute of Public Administration, 1981.

CORI, *Handbook for the Leaders of Religious Congregations: The Trusteeship of Catholic voluntary secondary schools*. Dublin: CORI, 1996.

Corish, P., *The Catholic Community in the Seventeenth and Eighteenth Centuries*, Dublin: Helicon, 1981.

Cross and Passion Sisters. Retrieved from www.cptryon.org/compassion/spr99/mmj.html.

Cullen Owens, R., *A Social History of Women in Ireland 1870–1970*, Dublin: Gill & Macmillan, 2005.

De La Salle Educational Mission. *Founder and History*. Retrieved from www.laselle2.org /English/Mission /Statement/mim.php.

De La Salle, J. B., *Meditations*. Maryland, US: Lasallian Publications, 1994.

Devas, F. C., *Mother Magdalen Taylor, Foundress of the Poor Servants of the Mother of God*, London: Burns Oates & Washbourne, 1927.

Doyle, E., *Leading the Way: Managing Voluntary Schools*, Dublin: Secretariat of Secondary Schools, 2000.

Drumm, M., *Address at the Launch of Le Chéile – a Catholic Schools Trust*, paper presented at the launch of the Le Chéile Trust, Dublin, 5 February 2010.

Elizabeth Prout. Retrieved from Cross and Passion website http://www.telegraph.co.uk/news/2205769/Nun-Elizabeth-Prout-could-become-saint.html.

Faithful Companions of Jesus, *Marie Madeleine*. Retrieved from www.fcjsisters.org/fcj.english/apirit/mmv.html.

Flaxman, R., *A Woman Styled Bold*, London: Darton, Longman and Todd, 1991.

Fuller, L., 'New Ireland and the Undoing of the Catholic Legacy: Looking Back to the Future' in Fuller, L., Littleton, J., & Maher, E. (eds.), *Irish and Catholic? Towards an Understanding of Identity*, pp. 86–89, Dublin: The Columba Press, 2006.

Gibbons, M., *The Life of Margaret Aylward*, London: Sands & Co., 1928.

Glendenning, D., *Education and the Law*, Dublin: Butterworths, 1999.

Grace, G., & O'Keefe, J. (eds.), *International Handbook on Catholic Education: Challenges for School Systems in the 21st century*, The Netherlands: Springer, 2007.

Groome, T. H., *What Makes Us Catholic*, San Francisco: Harper, 2003

History of Cross and Passion College, Kilcullen. Retrieved from http://www.cpckilcullen.com/www.cpckilcullen.com/history.html.

Holy Child Sisters. Cornelia Connelly. Retrieved from http://shcj.org/history_foundress.html.

Hyland, A., & Milne, K. (eds.), *Irish Educational Documents*, vol I, Dublin: Church of Ireland College of Education, 1992.

Kealy, M., *Dominican Education in Ireland 1820–1930*, Dublin: Irish Academic Press, 2007.

Kearns, B. *The Dominican Approach to Education* (Unpublished pamphlet), Internal Dominican congregational document.

Keenan, D., *The Catholic Church in Nineteenth Century Ireland*, Dublin: Gill and MacMillan, 1983.

Le Chéile Charter, Dublin: Le Chéile Trust, 2009.

Leonard, E., *Frances Taylor Mother Magdalen S.M.G.: A Portrait 1832–1900* Stoke-on-Trent: Brookes, 2005.

McLaughlin, T., O'Keefe, J., & O'Keeffe, B. (eds.), *The Contemporary Catholic School: Context, Identity and Diversity*, Oxon: Routledge Falmer, 1996.

Marie, Dom Antoine OSB, Letter of Saint Joseph Abbey on Claudine Thévenet. Retrieved from http://www.traditions-monastiques.net/site_abbaye /lettres/en/99 /zb70499141298.html, 7 April 1999.

Moody, T. W., & Martin, F. X. (eds.), *The Course of Irish History*, Cork: Mercier Press, 1967.

Murphy, A., *SHCJ and Ireland part 1: The First Irish sisters* (Internal SHCJ Congregational Document), 1996.

Murphy, A., *Handing on the Charism: Cornelia Connelly's Vision for Education* (Internal SHCJ Congregational Document), 2001.

Murphy, A., *In Search of a House in Ireland* (Internal SHCJ Congregational Document), 1998.

Nagle, C., *Religious of Christian education* (Internal RCE Congregational Document), 2008.

Neary, J., *John Baptist de La Salle* (Internal de La Salle Congregational Document), Alfred Calcutt fsc sources, 2008.

O'Flynn, K. M., *The Story Goes On* (Internal FCJ Congregational Document), 2009.

Orlandis, J., *A Short History of the Catholic Church* (Ediciones Rialp, S.A. Madrid 1985), trans. M. Adams, Four Courts Press, 1983.

Patrician Brothers' bicentenary history, *By the Narrow Gate*, Tullow: Patrician General Secretariat, 2008.

Pauline, Sr. M., *God Wills It*, Dublin: Browne and Nolan Ltd, 1959.

Prunty, J., *Holy Faith Secondary Schools* (Internal Congregational Document), 2008.

Prunty, J., *Founding years: The 'lay character' of the Holy Faith Congregation* (Internal Congregational Document), 2007.

Prunty, J., *Lady of Charity, Sister of Faith Margaret Aylward 1810–1889*, Dublin: Four Courts Press, 1999.

Religious of Jesus and Mary, *History of the Irish Province 1912–1991* (Internal Congregational Document), 1990.

Reynolds, E.E., *The Roman Catholic Church in England and Wales*, Wheat-hampstead: Clarke, 1973.

Reynolds, A.M., *'A woman who said yes', The Story of Elizabeth Prout (1820–1864)* (Internal Cross and Passion Congregational Document), 1998.

Scarisbrick, J.J., *Selly Park and Beyond*, Durham: The Sisters of Charity of St Paul the Apostle, 1997.

Schreck, A., *The Compact History of the Catholic Church*, Cincinnati: Servant Books, 2009.

Sisters of St Paul the Apostle (Internal Congregational Document), no author, provided by former archivist, Sr Phyllis Brady.

Sisters of the Cross and Passion, an international resource site for the passionist sisters. About our Founder, Elizabeth Prout, 2009. Retrieved from http://www.cptryon.org/scp/char.html.

St Louis Catholic Sisters. Retrieved from http://www.stlcatholicsisters.org.

St Louis Sisters. Retrieved from www.stlouissisters.org/history.html.

Stanislaus, Fr, *Life of the Viscountess De Bonault d'Houët*, London: Longmans Green & Co., 1916.

Strain, M.A., 'Elizabeth Prout, an extraordinary life,' in *Compass*, Spring, 1999, No. 56. New Jersey: Passionist Missionaries of Union City.

Taylor, M.M., *From Irish Homes and Irish Hearts*. London: Longmans Green and Co., 1867.

Teresa Mary, Philomena, Sylvester, Adrienne and Fionnuala, *Sisters of Jesus and Mary in Irish Province 1912–1921*. Private circulation document for Canonisation of Founder, Claudine Thévenet, 1993.

Tete, N., 'Catholic education in India: Challenge, response, and research,' in Grace, G., & O'Keefe, J. (eds.), *International Handbook of Catholic Education: Challenges for School Systems in the 21st Century* (pp. 683–94), The Netherlands: Springer, 2007.

Toppo, P. T., 'Catholic education and the church's concern for the marginal-ised: A view from India,' in Grace, G., & O'Keefe, J. (eds.), *International Handbook of Catholic Education: Challenges for School Systems in the 21st Century* (pp. 653–64), The Netherlands: Springer, 2007.

Torbert, W., *Why Educational Research has been so Uneducational: The Case for a New Model of Social Science based on Collaborative Inquiry,* San Francisco: John Wiley and Sons, 1981.

Tosh, J., *Why History Matters,* London: Palgrave Macmillan, 2008.

Towey, J., from original documents in holdings at Archives Centrales Generalice Rome, Diocesan Archives, Sligo, and de La Salle Prov-incialate Archives, Dublin, 2008.

Tracy, B., editorial in *Doctrine & Life, 59,* 6, Dublin: Dominican Publications, 2006.

Tuohy, D., 'Celebrating the past: Claiming the future,' in Grace, G., & O'Keefe, J. (eds.), *International Handbook of Catholic Education: Challenges for School Systems in the 21st Century* (pp. 269–90), The Netherlands: Springer, 2007.

Tuohy, D., 'Issues in Catholic education in Ireland,' in Woulfe, E., & Cassin, J. (eds.), *From Present to Future* (pp. 20–46), Dublin: Veritas, 2006.

Tuohy, D., *Leading Life to the Full,* Dublin: Veritas, 2005.

Walker, L. H., *The Purpose of his Will,* Galway: Patrician Brothers (Internal Congregational Document), 1981.

Wall, M., 'The age of the penal laws,' in Moody, T. W., & Martin, F. X. (eds.), *The Course of Irish History* (pp. 217–31), Cork: Mercier Press, 1967.

Wanden, K., & Birch, L., 'Catholic schools in New Zealand,' in Grace, G., & O'Keefe, J. (eds), *International Handbook of Catholic education: Challenges for School Systems in the 21st Century* (pp. 847–70), The Netherlands: Springer, 2007.

Wheately, M., *Finding Our Way, Leadership for an Uncertain Time,* San Francisco: Berrett Koehler Publishers Inc., 2005.

Wheately, M., *Turning to One Another,* San Francisco: Barrett Koehler, 2002.

Wheately, M., *Leadership and the New Science,* San Francisco: Berrett-Koehler, 1999.

Wheately, M., & Kellner-Rougers, M., *A Simpler Way,* San Francisco: Barrett Koehler, 1999.

Whitehead, J.D., & Whitehead, E., *The Emerging Laity, Returning Leadership to the Community of Faith*, New York: Doubleday & Company Inc., 1986.

Wieczorek, W., 'Challenges for Catholic education in Poland post 1989/91,' in Grace, G., & O'Keefe, J. (eds.), *International Handbook of Catholic Education: Challenges for School Systems in the 21st Century* (pp. 501–18), The Netherlands: Springer, 2007.

Williams, K., 'The common school and the Catholic school: A response to the work of T.H. Mc Laughlin,' *International Studies in Catholic Education*, 2(1), 9–36, 2010.

Williams, K., *Faith and the Nation*, Dublin: Dominican Publications, 2005.

Winter, R., *Learning from Experience*, London: The Falmer Press, 1989.

Wirtz Molezun, M.P., *Religious life for this 'other possible world'*, paper presented at the Union Internazionale Superiore Generall (UISG), Rome (No. 1322006), 2007.

Woulfe, E., & Cassin, J. (eds.), *From Present to Future*, Dublin: Veritas, 2007.